Growing Up in the Bronx

A heartwarming account of seven children and their hard-pressed parents during the 1930's and 1940's

Christina Lynch-Hilgenberg

Seattle

CreateSpace

An Amazon Company

Seattle

Copyright 2015 by Christina Lynch-Hilgenberg

All rights reserved, including the right to reproduce this book or portions thereof in any form whatsoever.

For information, please contact the author.

First Edition May 2015

ISBN-13: 978-1499256932 (CreateSpace-Assigned)
ISBN-10: 1499256930

For my family

4

This collection of short stories is an attempt to recapture experiences of my childhood spent in the beautiful Bronx during the Depression and the World War II and post-war eras, which are dear to my heart.

These memories must be preserved because they can no longer be experienced by anyone again as the wonderful places and friends I loved as a child are no longer there and will never be seen again.

Some people who have grown up in areas of the U.S. that, fortunately for them, never seem to change, that have moved away, can go back to their roots and relive old acquaintances and experiences once again, those places where they lived as a child, and relive those memories.

They can visit their old schools and meet with their old classmates and childhood companions; that means a great deal to people.

My friend Doris and I used to love to take long walks on a summer's day from our neighborhood on 160th Street and Melrose Avenue to places as far away as the Loew's Paradise movie theater near Fordham Road and the Grand Concourse.

The Grand Concourse was the most beautiful street in the Bronx and we used to admire the beautiful and elegant apartment houses. Most had doormen out front who were very polite and would greet us as we passed by. We would get glimpses of the gorgeous courtyards filled with flowers of all descriptions.

Having grown up in the apartment houses in the Bronx most of which were very well kept, bright and livable, we always wondered what it would be like to live in one of the Concourse houses.

LOUIS CHARLES GAERTH

My mother's father was Louis Charles Gaerth. He was born in New York City on October 30, 1871 to Charles Gaerth and Anna Schneider. He had a horse drawn wagon from which he sold cigars. My mother told me that he would often take her on his rounds with him. These were happy memories for her.

His family came to America from Alsace-Lorraine on the German side of the border with France. He married my Grandmother, Margaret Barry on May 29, 1898. They had three children and lived in the same apartment building with the Barry Grandparents. Margaret died after the death of her third child. My mother and her brother then went to live with their grandparents the Barry's but saw their father every day. He remarried a widow named Ella. They took my mother to an apartment on 160th Street. She showed it to me once. She cried so much for her grandparents that they allowed her to go back to them. She lived there until her marriage.

Louis died on November 6, 1922. He had a heart condition and worked in the shipping department of their tobacco business. His oldest brother sold cigars. A long time ago I found a record of a family member who stated in a census that the family was in the "see-gar" business. It took me a minute of saying it fast to realize that it meant "cigar."

MY MOTHER'S STEPMOTHER

Grandma, my mother's stepmother, was an elegant looking lady. I was about five or six years old when she died and I was very sad as I loved her very much. I can remember Mama crying and that Uncle Larpse, the undertaker, had been called. I was sitting on his lap as he consoled me.

After my grandfather died, she remarried a man we called Uncle Bill. From what I remember he too was very elegant and he was very tall. He was also blind. When we visited their apartment on 161st and Brook Avenue we had to be very careful not to move anything. They had two rocking chairs and a buffet; everything was in its place. As a little child I found this very fascinating.

One time she took me into her bedroom and showed me some of her pictures and other mementos. I remember her visiting us when we lived on 158th street and bringing ice cream. She always looked beautiful.

MY MOTHER

Florence Loretta Gaerth was my mother. She was well taken care of by her grandparents. But, I also think that perhaps she was somewhat lonely because she once told me she grew up with all old people. She loved them very much and they really watched over her.

I can imagine that she was thrilled when she met my father's family. He was the last to get married and they were a big clannish group. They welcomed her and loved her very much. She was thrilled with all the brothers and sisters, and the many children. My aunt Mary and she were like sisters throughout their whole lives. She led a very social life. They went to all the Broadway and Vaudeville Shows. They also went to the shows in Harlem where they were very welcome at that time, not to mention their frequent visits to my father's speakeasies!!!

My mother's grandmother, Johanna Mahoney Barry, passed away before she had the chance to meet the Lynches. I often wondered what her reaction would have been to this colorful family!

THE LYNCH SWIMMERS

The Lynch Family loved to swim and they were excellent swimmers. They liked to go to "Rockaway Beach" and even Aunt Mary, who was a big woman, was a very strong swimmer.

One time I asked my father how they all learned to swim, because there wouldn't have been a swimming pool down in Manhattan where they lived. He explained to me that when they considered one of the children old enough to swim, they took them down to the East River and threw them in with the dog. The children in the neighborhood all swam in the East River. I asked him how old they were because I was horrified, and he said, "oh about five or seven"!!! I said "you would never throw us in the East River would you?" He said "Of course not, but you have to realize these were very difficult times, and you had to be strong to survive." He also told me, they never had shoes in the winter and he and his brothers would carry bags down to the railroad when the coal trains came in. They just filled their bags with the coal, or everyone at home would freeze. They were given a loaf of bread every day, for attending school. The only times they had meat was fried bologna. At the time I thought he was just kidding me, but as I got older I realized what a hard life he had and it made me sad.

Re: Frosty, Aunt Mary's husband. Aunt Mary called him that behind his back because he rarely spoke to anyone, which was totally foreign to her personality! One time Peggy almost called him Frosty, and Aunt Mary was waving wildly behind him to signal Peggy to be quiet, that this was a nickname that he didn't know about!!

MAMA AND DADDY

One pretty sunny day in late June 1920, Daddy was standing on the corner of 101st Street and Third Avenue in Manhattan talking to a lady he knew from the neighborhood. A very pretty, well-dressed young lady came by and said hello to Daddy's friend. Daddy wanted to know who this girl was and wanted to be introduced to her. In 1920 you couldn't just ask someone out, you had to be properly introduced. Ann McGill said, "That's Florrie Gaerth and she will not go out with you. She is only 21 years old and you are too old for her" (Daddy was 30.) "At one time she considered being a nun. She is the nicest girl in the neighborhood and you own two speakeasies." (I didn't know about the speakeasies until many years later when my cousin, Jack Lynch, told me about them)

But, Daddy insisted upon the introduction and bet Ann $100 that Mama would go out with him. Four months later they were married at St. Simon Stock's Church in the Bronx. They moved into an apartment in Throgg's Neck and Ann McGill paid dad the $100!

THE PAIN OF THE DEPRESSION

Recently I asked my oldest sister, Peggy, if we ever went to sleep hungry. I was interested because I never felt like we were hungry. There was always something we could eat even if it was the old Irish staple, a potato, or bread and butter which we put sugar on for a treat, and Mama made oatmeal raisin cookies. I felt we had a good home and so I guess the Depression didn't seem so terrible to me. Peggy told me that when I was born, I had to sleep in a wash basket because Jimmy was till in the crib. She also told me that once when I was a little baby I was very hungry and there was no milk in the house. They tried to give me tea and I was crying hysterically because of the hunger. She said she was crying also and that my mother was crying her eyes out and had a bad attack of indigestion from all the stress.

My father decided to go down to Uncle Tommy to get some money, but he didn't have the five cents for the fare. We lived two blocks away from the 156th Street El Station so he had to walk about 67 blocks from the Bronx to 89th Street and Third Avenue in Manhattan to meet with Uncle Tommy to get the money to feed his family. He took the train back and went right to the grocery store. It broke my heart to hear this story as I began to realize the stress all parents went through during this time and they really never let us know how bad it was.

When my father had all his money in the 1920's he took care of everyone who was in need and during the Depression his brothers thankfully helped him.

I remember one day I was out with my mother and I saw a woman sitting on all of her furniture on the sidewalk with her children. She was crying. I asked my mother what was wrong. She said they were probably moving and waiting for the moving van. I couldn't understand why she would be crying. I guess Mama thought I was much too young to learn the ugly parts of life and said she probably missed her friends. But I soon figured it out for myself and realized they were being put out of their apartment for not paying their rent. This was not uncommon at this time.

Another thing I found very disturbing during the Depression was when men would come into our backyard and play an instrument while they sang a popular song. People would then throw coins out to them. This absolutely horrified me and made me cry.

One time when my father had a lot of money he saw an old woman sitting on her furniture out on her sidewalk and crying. Men were actually carrying her things and dumping them on the sidewalk. He got out of his car and asked to speak to the person in charge. The man said she owed three month's rent. My father was furious. He paid her rent and three months in advance and told him if she needed more he was to find my father. He told the man if he ever came by again, and he surely would and this poor old woman was in this situation the man would be lying in the street in very bad shape. I just don't know how anyone could do such a terrible thing to an old woman who had no one.

I think the government started paying rent around 1934 because people stayed in their homes and we didn't see them on the streets any more.

OUR UNCLE TOMMY

Uncle Tommy was my father's oldest brother. He was the oldest in the family of twelve children. He was born in England and came to this country at around five years of age. All of our uncles and aunts were wonderful. They loved us and we knew it. In many families when grownups came to visit, the children were sent off to another room. Not with us. We had time to sit and talk with them and hear their stories. Uncle Tommy was a very husky strong man who looked bigger than life to us. He actually was not tall, but he gave that appearance because of his personality.

He was a building inspector in New York City and had a badge that he wore when he was at work. But, when he came to se us he would put it on his suit jacket and it looked so big and impressive to us. We thought he was running the city. He also was a Crossing Guard for the school crossing on Third Avenue and 89th Street where our cousins, Uncle Larpse's children had to cross to get to school. When they appeared on the corner he would blow his whistle and stop all traffic. Green light or red light it didn't matter to him, nothing moved. He would walk over to where the children were waiting and place his arm in theirs and march across Third Avenue then blow his whistle and traffic would flow as usual. They were so embarrassed and had to endure the same ritual on the way home.

I know that Uncle Tommy took care of us during the Depression. It seemed he was always there when something was needed, especially Thanksgiving and Christmas, but many other times also.

He was another one who always made soup and always had a large pot of soup on the stove. I guess he must have given most of it to his neighbors. He couldn't possibly eat it all. My cousin, Jack Lynch, went to high school in that area, but lived in the Bronx. Uncle Tommy wouldn't hear of him having his lunch anywhere else while he had so much soup. So Jack spent many wonderful lunches and heard many exciting stories while at Uncle Tommy's house. I wish I had spent more time with him.

The last time I saw him, my father sent my friend Doris, and me down to his apartment to invite him to have Sunday dinner. They hadn't seen each other for a while and Uncle Larpse had recently died and Daddy wanted to see more of this brother who had been so good to us.

Doris and I took the Third Avenue El and found his apartment. He was happy to see me and said of course he would be there and he looked forward to it. But, before the week was up he got sick and was taken to the hospital where he died a short time later of, (I think) stomach cancer. We were all so sad, especially Daddy.

Whenever he saw us he gave us each $1.00 I will never forget him because he always made a big deal out of everything and was so much fun to be around. My brother, Eddie, was so much like him.

DADDY'S FRIENDS

My father was always very fussy about how he looked. He didn't have many clothes during the Depression, but they were well taken care of and he always looked nice. My dad had a friend named Willie Winkle and being New Yorkers he was called Wee Willie Winkle. He was small. My father was only 5 feet 8 inches and Willie was smaller than that. He brought each of us a souvenir from Florida. I remember I was thrilled with a doll made completely of seashells. She had elastic in her arms and legs and I could move her all around. She had a seashell face and a larger seashell for a big hat. I was very pleased because no one else had one except Bootsie, my younger sister. That is about all I remember about the visit so I must have been quite young.

The next two characters I will never forget. They were from the old days and came quite often. Tom Comisky I think usually came in the summer, but may have come other times too. I just remember he always had a straw hat and a fancy cane. Daddy and Mr. Comisky taught me how to tap dance to all the old tunes they loved so much. I would be in the middle with one on each side. I seem to think the other kids took off. They were not very impressed with all of this nonsense. But, I loved to dance and had a ball. Then Mr. Comisky did a dance with just me. We danced to:

> "While strolling through the park one day
>
> In the merry, merry month of May
>
> I was taken by surprise
>
> By a pair of roughish eyes
>
> And sure she did steal my heart away."

I of course was the girl with roughish eyes waltzing past him and breaking his heart. He then had a fabulous finish. He would flip his hat off his head and have it roll down his arm to catch in his hand.

I really wanted to be a dancer and thought I could be on Broadway. Ha, like Daddy saw that in my future, but he let me have my fun while I could. They were marvelous times.

A man called "Red Shirt" simply because he always wore a red shirt also visited quite a bit. He wore plain red, red plaid, red checked or any red he could find. He was a lot of fun and as big as a lumber jack. But we were always a little bit leery of him as there was a story we once heard about him. During Prohibition the whole crew was having a party in a fifth floor apartment somewhere and someone said something Red Shirt took offense to and he grabbed the man and hung him upside down by the ankles out the window. The other kids were interested in him, but we all sat with our eyes popping out and our mouths closed very tight should we say something wrong and find ourselves hanging out the window by our ankles. Things could get pretty exciting at our house.

When Bootsie was a baby we lived on 160th Street near Morris Avenue, in a private house. We had an apple tree, that didn't bear any fruit that year. The children would wake up every morning and run to the window to see if some apples had grown yet. They were very disappointed each morning, so one night while they were sleeping; Daddy tied apples all over the tree. When we woke up the next morning and looked out the window we were all so excited!!! That's the kind of father he was.

Our next move was to 158th Street, near Morris Avenue. My brother Eddie was always making faces and we called him the little weasel. He was always afraid of getting cheated. When Daddy dished out our dinner, Eddie always counted what was on our plates, even the peas

I thought my Aunt Jenny was my Uncle Tommy's wife, but when he died in 1947 we went to his funeral and I saw a lovely distinguished woman, two men and one young woman. I asked Mama who these people were, and she replied, that's Uncle Tommy's wife and his three children. I said, " I thought Aunt Jenny was his wife" and Mama said; shush, shush, shush, I'll explain it later." Of course she never did because we never talked about such things. You just got old enough to figure it out for yourself. The cousins were William, the oldest, who looked just like his mother, Edmund who looked just like the Lynch's and Eleanor who was very lovely. They were great to us and made such a fuss over us.

PUPPY

My brother Buddy loved Aunt Mary, and she was crazy about him! He was the son she never had. She had a little dog named Puppy and he loved that dog! He used to take the trolley often to visit her and Puppy in the Bronx and Puppy used to fuss all day when Buddy was coming. Aunt Mary always knew by how the dog acted that Buddy would visit that day.

BABIES-BUGGIES-BIKES

When we were little girls growing up in the Bronx during the Depression we always had baby dolls to play with. Some of the children even had buggies for their dolls or the really lucky ones had three wheeler bikes.

When my father went to find us an apartment on 160th Street, he told Joe, the janitor, that we had four children in school. Joe wasn't too pleased when he saw seven children march into the apartment. He asked my father what was going on. Daddy told him we did have four children in school, but we also had three at home that he forgot to mention. He also explained that he could be assured that we would never cause any trouble at all.

We were very well behaved children and Joe soon learned to love us. One day he came up to the front of the house with a baby buggy and a three wheeled bicycle and asked me if I would like to have it. Someone had moved away and had left it. I was absolutely thrilled to own a carriage and a bike. They were in excellent condition. Mama immediately made me a mattress, a pillow and a beautiful blanket to match. She also made all new clothes for my doll. My friends and Bootsie and I walked that buggy up and down the street all day. We would only stop to take care of our babies or to have a tea party. The O'Reilley girls gave us their beautiful tea set for they felt that they had out grown it. They were real china and about one third the size of an adult set. Mama made lemonade and we set up our tea party on the front stoop which is what we called the front steps leading into our apartment house. When we weren't playing dolls we were wildly flying up and down the sidewalk on our street.

Joe sold my mother an electric sewing machine for $5.00. She must have made thousands of dollars of clothes on that machine. In later years Peggy and Buddy bought her a brand new machine in a cabinet. Buddy even sewed on it. I remember he could hardly wait to get it put together so he could try it out. I think Peggy may even have it now. Joe even gave Buddy the job of washing down the stairs once a week. I don't know how thrilled he was with that, but it brought money into the house.

I watch my grandchildren now and they don't play with dolls for very long. As soon as they are old enough to play Barbies, the lose interest in the dolls. They seem to only want a bike when they are old enough for a big two wheeler. They are so caught up in video games they don't seem to play. I loved growing up in the Bronx. The street was just teaming with kids of all ages playing together. I wouldn't trade those times for anything.

BUCKETS AND BASEBALL

Buddy had a job washing down the hallways in the apartment building. The stairs and landings were marble and had to be mopped every Saturday. Buddy started on the top floor. He had the keys to the empty apartments in the building. He would fill his bucket on the top floor and work his way down to the third floor. Apartment 3A was empty so he would change his water there. One time as he was changing the water he glanced into the kitchen mirror over the sink and saw two people sleeping in bed. Someone had moved into the apartment during the week no one had told him. He grabbed his bucket and got out as fast as he could.

Buddy had a job to earn some extra money selling The Sporting News at Yankee Stadium. Some Irish men from Chicago asked him his name and I guess Dan Lynch was the good Irish name they wanted to hear, because they gave him the seat next to the Yankee dugout. He spent the entire game with the Yankees and the beloved Lou Gehrig. Buddy didn't sell many papers that day, but came home to excitedly tell about his big adventure.

SKATES AND SCOOTERS

When we were growing up in the Bronx in the 1930's, the only wheels we had were roller skates. The skates came with a key to adjust the clamps and we always tied the key around our necks usually with some string or an old shoelace. Many children didn't have skates so we were always borrowing back and forth. The skate key was so important that you never took it off while you were skating. It was used to lengthen or shorten the skates or to hold them onto your toes. One Christmas all four of the youngest children in our family got roller skates. I remember we flew through the streets with great abandon for hours.

When the metal wheels were worn down the skates were dismantled and attached to a wooden fruit crate and made into a pushcart or scooter.

Our brothers made scooters for us and we flew down the streets with the wind blowing in our faces, and feeling very adventurous. Traffic wasn't a problem as few people could afford cars.

Doing errands on skates was not only faster but the owners of the stores where we shopped didn't even mind if we entered the well-worn wide planked floors covered with sawdust. In High School, all of our friends went to an indoor roller-skating rink where we rented real high shoe roller skates. They had an organ player who sat high up in a glass case in the wall. It was so wonderful to skate round and round to the glorious music of that era. One Christmas, Bootsie and I got beautiful pure white skates. We also got metal boxes to keep them in. Mama made beautiful blue corduroy skirts with fancy red lining. It was so wonderful and we were so surprised.

PENNY CANDY

When we were little children during the Depression, Daddy would give each of us one penny every day so we could go around to Gray's Candy Store on Melrose Avenue. We had to wait until the older ones got home from school to take us. I remember one day Daddy gave the four little ones their penny in the morning. We put them in a safe place for when the other children came home. Later in the afternoon, he said to me: "Dena here is your penny". I reminded him that that he had already given me my penny and I dug it out of my pocket to show him. I'll never forget what he said next. "Dena what a good girl you are to be so honest. Just for that here is another special penny for you." As an adult, I looked back and realized he was testing me. One of our family rules was that we always had to tell the truth. He was so happy that I didn't try to put one over on him. Fat chance of that ever happening! I would never tell a lie to my parents. I saved those for the priests!

Gray's Candy Store looked like all the old pictures you see in the old movies. Outside was a wooden sort of hutch with a back on it, and slats in the front to hold the papers. The papers were delivered at 10:00 at night. A big delivery truck would throw all the papers bound in rope onto the sidewalk and everyone would be waiting for the evening paper. The papers also came in the morning for the people on their way to work. The leftover ones were put in the top of the hutch and the others in the bottom, which had some shelves and two doors. Daddy let me go for the papers because I loved it. I liked all the people around and the paper boy yelling "get your paper, get your paper, all the latest news."

When you went inside the store, on the right there were coke bottles in a cooler, and magazines on shelves. On the left was the counter where you could get all kinds of ice-cream and sodas. In the back on the right were two phone booths. Next to that were sloped shelves with open boxes of candy. Poor Mr. Gray had a lot to take in, especially at the candy counter. Sometimes there would be ten kids hanging around trying to make their big decision. He needed to keep a sharp eye on their hands and pockets.

My mother liked Necco wafers and I would love to buy them for her once a week. She always looked so surprised like this never happened before.

Mary was the one we had to keep a watch on. They had a box of oval chocolate covered creams. The inside was white cream with a few pink ones in the box too. Mary seemed so lucky to get a pink one all the time. A pink one would give you an extra one and she would give it to one of us. Then one day I noticed that she would pick up a candy and stick her fingernail in the bottom. If the filling was white she put it back and chose another one, if it was pink she would give it to one of us to say we found a pink one. I was horrified and didn't take any more of her candies. One day Mr. Gray said: "You Lynch kids sure have the luck of the Irish.'" I was so glad when I was old enough to go by myself.

STREET SMARTS

Daddy started teaching us street smarts at a very early age. We were permitted to play outside of our apartment house at about five years of age, I think. By the time Daddy was fourteen years old he had lost five siblings and his mother. He would tell us about them and would always cry. I think he lived in terrible fear that he would lose one of us that is why he kept such close watch of us at all ages. I know now that he would never have survived losing Mama or one of us.

Here are his rules:

Always be aware of who was around us.

Never go near a stranger.

Walk down the middle of the sidewalk so you would not be too close to the houses where there were alleyways and cars at the curb. We lived in a nice building. You walked up four steps and then one more before you entered a very nice vestibule where all the mailboxes were. If we saw anyone we did not know in there looking at the mailboxes, we were not to enter but cross to a different building until the person left.

If someone we didn't know entered the building after we did, we were to press our bell and keep our finger on it. We lived on the main floor so Daddy would come flying out.

We were never to stand near the train tracks on the subway or the elevated trains, but back against the wall.

If we were at the movies and a man or a boy came and sat next to us we were to change our seat. There were always plenty of seats for people to sit and no one needed to sit right next to you.

At the movies we should always sit next to the exit, so we could get out in case of fire or anything else.

We were all very aware and alert. As a matter of fact these instructions actually saved my life on two occasions and Mary's once. I will tell those stories later.

When we started to go out working my mother was given the task of warning us what we should be aware of on the trains. We took the trains to High School where everyone was going north, but now we would be heading into Manhattan where we would be on very crowded trains. The Trains were packed and you could hardly move. So Mama told me I might want to start carrying a hat pin. I said "a hat pin? I don't even wear a hat." As delicately as possible she explained that I might have to use it on some man who might take advantage and inappropriately touch me. I was absolutely horrified. I went right out that night and bought an umbrella with a very sharp tip on it. Instead of holding it down, I held it sideways under my arm. Actually, it had quite a wide berth. No one came near me. I guess I had that Irish look that said, "Don't even think of it."

Soon after that someone told me about the Central Train that ran just a few blocks from my house to Grand Central Station in twenty minutes. You always got a seat and it was worth the extra money. No one had to carry an umbrella unless it was raining.

STREET SMARTS, CONTINUED

Daddy's rules save both Mary and Dena:

When I was about five or six we were permitted to play outside the front of the house. Many children gathered on someone's stoop. This day I came out of the apartment when I encountered a man standing not three or four feet near me on the stairs that went up to the other floors. He asked me if I could show him where the Rapp's lived. Of course they lived on the top floor. I am sure he looked through the mailboxes for someone that far up. He said he had to deliver a paper to them and would give me ten cents if I helped him. At first ten cents sounded pretty good, but I knew Daddy would somehow find out that I had not obeyed him. Suddenly I got this terrible dark frightening feeling come over me and I knew I had to get away from him. Instead of running back into the apartment, I ran out of the building and hid in the bushes in Mr. Butler's house right across the street and hid until he came out and went up the street. I should have run in the house, but I was afraid he would grab me before I made it to the door. After he left, I ran home and told Daddy what had happened. Daddy went wild. He could not understand why I didn't come in the house instead of letting this man get away. He dragged me all over the neighborhood, but I couldn't find him. Daddy realized the guy was going to get someone else, but I didn't understand why he was upset with me. A good thing we didn't find him because Daddy would have beaten him terribly and he would have ended up in jail. He wasn't a big man, but he was very strong and if someone was after children there would be no stopping him.

It bothered him so much that he brought it up often and made me feel guilty that the man might find some other girl. One day we were in the kitchen when he started it again and Peggy came to my rescue. She said, "Daddy, why don't you leave her alone? She's just a little girl and you are hurting her every time you bring it up. Why can't you just be thankful she is here?

Think of how we would all be suffering if she hadn't gotten away. "Daddy said, "Peggy, you are right. Dena, come over here and let me give you a hug. You are a very brave girl and none of this was your fault. I promise you I will never bring it up again." And he never did.

When I was a teenager I used to love to go down to Third Avenue and window shop. There were so many shops from 156th Street on down to 149th Street. From 156th Street up to 160th Street there were small shops that closed early. One evening when I got to about 157th Street I realized I was being followed. It dawned on me that this man seemed to be everywhere that I was. I decided to cross Third Avenue to see what would happen, and sure enough he crossed too. I was really scared because the streets were getting darker and I had to go up a side street to get off the Avenue, but they were dark with no one on them. I said to myself, "Okay Dena, think. You have to have a plan for 160th street because you can't go any further that that. The Police Station was nearby, but it would be a good run past all the cars they parked in front of it. I was all set to run when suddenly Mrs. Bissonette walked out of the last store and I told her how happy I was to see her because the man was following me. We looked back and he was walking the other way.

Mary called one night from a drugstore on Third Avenue because she was being followed. Daddy told her to stay in the store and he would be right down to get her.

He grew up in one of those poor immigrant neighborhoods down in Manhattan. They were rough places and had lots of rough kids. He was very bright and knew he had to protect us no matter where we lived. I am so grateful for that because we were all very alert, not afraid, but thinkers of how to get out of a bad situation.

My father and his three brothers were all very bright. It is unfortunate they weren't able to get a good education. I am sure they could have been in politics because not only were they sharp, but also had the personality. We all loved them and they loved us and showed it.

MARKING IT DOWN

We did all of our shopping on Melrose Avenue where the store owners knew us. This was because we rarely could pay for what we were purchasing and had to ask them to "mark it down" which meant to buy it on credit. When the Government check came on the first of the month we would pay them what we could so we always had a running tab. These people were very hard working and bless them because they kept many of us alive during the terrible Depression. There weren't any jobs and the people were desperate.

We had Tony, the green grocer, who was always willing to mark it down for us. He and his wife would put all of the big boxes of fruits and vegetables out on the sidewalk in front of the store and take them back in at night. They also had a back room where they kept the vegetables fresh. The inside of the store was filled with all kinds of delicious food. The floor was old wooden planks and had straw all over it. It was always freezing in the winter. They had a little wood burning stove, but they always had to wear sweaters and heavy jackets. Their gloves had the tips of the fingers cut out of them so they could handle the cash or most probably mark it down. Sometimes they would give us an apple on our way out.

When the Depression was over and the older children started to work my mother would send me every Saturday to pay Tony something on our bill. When I made the last payment he told me to tell my parents we were the only ones who paid him back every penny we owed him. That made me feel very proud and I knew I would never cheat anyone in my life.

We also had the Italian butchers. They were two brothers who had a very nice store just around the corner. It too had straw on the floor. I used to wonder why all the stores had straw on their floors, but never asked. We were very careful not to ask about things that were none of our business. I would ask them for two pounds of soup bones and be sure to have some meat on them. I might also get a pound of soup meat. I of course asked to have them mark it down. They had a big long bologna hanging from the ceiling and would get a huge knife out and cut off a big piece of bologna and hand it to me. It was the best bologna I ever tasted.

We could also mark down delicious food from the German Deli. Rye bread, potato salad, pickles, ham and cheese, smoked white fish, pickled herring and even two bottles of beer for Daddy. We paid them more every month because their bill was larger and if you didn't pay I doubt you could keep the tab going for very long.

We also had the Italian Store where you bought only pasta, bread or sauces to make spaghetti, etc. There was no marking it down at this store. The woman was obese and she sat right in the front window where she could keep an eye on everyone who came in. The walls had drawers in them with glass panels so you could see what you were getting. We always got one and a half pounds of spaghetti and a delicious loaf of Italian bread. (We would have already gotten the chopped meat for the sauce at the butchers, where we could mark it down). She would haul herself up and grab the spaghetti and weigh it. She never made a mistake. It was always exactly one and a half pounds. We were smart enough to watch to see if she kept her finger on the scale. She would then place the spaghetti on some butcher paper and then tie it up with a spool of light rope that was attached to the ceiling and ran through a pulley which ran down to her counter. Then we would get either the round or the long Italian bread which was unbelievably delicious. If it was the long bread you just couldn't stop yourself from tearing off a hunk to eat on the way home. She also had a big tub of butter and if we had a little extra money we would ask for one pound. She had a scoop which she dipped in the butter and as usual it was exactly one pound. I wonder now if somehow she had a trick scale. Anyway, you paid your money and off you went.

I used to wave to her as I passed the window as I wanted her to like me. She was scary and you didn't want her for an enemy. You never knew about those Italians who make you pay cold hard cash.

You couldn't mark down at the German Bakery or the German Wurst Store. The Germans didn't trust the Irish scoundrels.

THE CHINA MAN

There was a Chinese Laundry on our block. I had one friend whose parents had enough money to send their laundry out. I loved when we went to bring it to them and to pick it up. It was a very small store and it fascinated me. The workers were all Chinese, and they all wore white tops and white skirts. They had long stringy braids all the way down their backs. The Chinese workers had a couple of ironing boards and big heavy irons. The cords for the irons were strung through the ceiling and strapped with metal coils so they didn't fray. There were shelves on the walls with the wash that was ready to be picked up. They hardly spoke any English when you handed them your ticket. I was really quite young and a bit afraid of them, as they were so foreign to me. The girls would find your laundry package and the man would hand it over to you after he added the amount you owned with an abacus. They were all so serious. Believe me you would hear, "No Tikee, No Shirtee" if you didn't have your ticket with you. They were such hard workers and it was so hot in that tiny place. When we were older, the old people retired and the younger ones took care of everything. They were very Americanized and not nearly as much fun.

THE JEW

I do not mean that in any derogatory way. He was a Jewish peddler who came around the neighborhood from the 1930's to about the early 1960's and he was always known as "The Jew." He knew that that was what he was called and as long as his business was prospering he didn't care. He would sell various items from his car and you would pay him so much every two weeks when he came around again to collect and hopefully sell some more items to you. I know it's hard to believe today, but he would come to the door and you would say hello to Mr. Paeger and then go into the other room and call out, "Mom, the Jew is here."

My mother did not have "The Jew" during the Depression because she could not pay out the few dollars she would owe him, but in the later forties when some extra money was coming in and she had not bought anything for the house for so many years she decided she would pick up some things like curtains or sheets or whatever we needed. Our Aunt Mary had "The Jew" forever and sent him down to Mama. Mr. Paeger was his name. The only way I knew that was his name, was because Aunt Mary gave him such a hard time every time he came to her house and spent so much time arguing with him and tormenting him that her grandson thought he was one of the uncles and called him Uncle Paeger. Her grandson was the only one who didn't know he was the "The Jew." She was just such a character that she would try not to pay him the money due that week or try to "Jew" him down. She had the money and he knew it, so he would eventually get paid. I am surprised he even went to see my mother thinking she was like Aunt Mary. What a surprise when he had an angel for a customer.

One time I went to visit my mother and she had a new bedspread which of course came from "The Jew." She was very careful about how much she bought, but there were lots of things she wanted to fix up in the apartment. I was living in a garden apartment in New Jersey at the time and the next week I saw Mama again she had a bedspread and matching curtains for me. Now I had an account with "The Jew" and I didn't even live in the Bronx.

When we moved to Utah the only job Huey could get was a job with the Jewel Tea Co. He came home and told me he would be delivering merchandise from a truck, on account, every two weeks. I said, "WE CAME ALL THE WAY OUT HERE AND NOW <u>YOU</u> ARE <u>THE JEW</u>!"

One of my very favorite cousins who was like an older sister to me married "A Jew." (Not to be confused with "The Jew.") Sidney Solomon Beck was a Bronx fireman and everyone loved him. So I called Gicki up one day and told her Sid should be happy because we now had another Jew in the family. When I explained how it came about we both laughed and laughed.

ROGOFF'S PICKLES

Believe it or not, we lived right next to a Pickle Factory. Buddy used to get upset with us because we called it a factory. Actually barrels and barrels of pickles were stored in the building while the pickles settled in the brine.

It was a great little building and the pickles smelled so good. Because of the barrels, the aroma was not too strong until the men came to get the barrels and then it was wonderful. The truck would pull up to the door and roll them to the ramp onto the truck. First they would pry open the lid of each one and test them. That's when they were bombarded by the children. We would gather around the door and all of us would be saying "Can I have a pickle, Can I have a pickle?" The poor guys would tell us these had to be sold and they were responsible for them. However, they couldn't turn us away and each one got a big fat juicy pickle. Oh, that was as good as any ice cream cone in those days. The next day the pickle men would come with a whole new bunch of barrels and roll them into the building until they were ready to be removed and we would have something to look forward to as we knew they were coming back for them.

Buddy was funny. He liked us to get everything right like when we called it a factory, he said factories made things like clothes, etc. Of course that was foolish because we did it even more.

One day I came home from the movies and he asked me what I saw. I told him the name of the movie and added that I had seen the "Coming Attractions." Well, that really was a great one to pull on him! He explained to me that I saw the "preview of the coming attractions." The movies would come next week. I insisted it said in big letters coming attractions. He kept at it until he thought I got it. Of course the next week I came home and announced to him with great pride "Guess what I saw? The coming attractions."

Buddy didn't like being poor or living in such a small apartment. If you wanted to take a bath it was important to make a big announcement about it in case someone had to use the bathroom. He made his announcement and then everyone said I have to go. I am laughing now because I can still see him about half and hour later standing in the hallway with his towel over his arm and his soap in his hand with a look I can't even describe.

We knew he would be the first one to leave. After the war he was offered a job in Texas and was gone. He did miss us because he wrote every week. He got married and I am pretty sure he and Joan moved down to Texas.

He used to tell Peggy that Melrose Avenue wasn't the only place to live in this world and he wanted to move someplace in the country and have a house. She was crazy about New York and still is. Well, he left, pickles and all, but we were always in his heart because despite living in the Bronx, he still loved us.

THE THREE YOUNGEST LYNCH CHILDREN

Jimmie was the sweetest and nicest little boy. We all loved him. I especially missed him when he started school. We were really good friends and he was so nice to me. We didn't go to kindergarten but started in the first grade at age six. We then started school every six months not like today when they start in September and go through to June.

Jimmie was a little thick headed Irish boy and one day when he was supposed to be in school he turned up at home. My father asked him what he was doing home in the middle of the day and Jimmy replied, "The teacher poked me in the ribs with her pencil, so I left and came home and I am not going back anymore. She has no right to do that to me." I was thrilled because I thought he would be able to play a game with me. Of course Daddy wasn't so thrilled and wanted to know why he was poked. I don't remember what the problem was, but Daddy marched him right back to straighten this whole thing out and Jimmie ended up apologizing to his teacher. She was frantic because she had lost one of her students.

FIFTH GRADE

We entered Fifth Grade and of course got a new teacher. We were all a little afraid because she was known as a very strict person. Her name was Mrs. Carew. I will never forget her because I was her pet. I don't know why, but she really liked me. Maybe it was because Mama made sure we always looked nice before we went to school. She was a very good teacher and we learned a lot in her class.

However, I did get upset with her one day as she started at the front desk and asked the children what their father did for a living. Most of the children were from poor Italian families and who knows what they were up to. The first boy stood up and said his father was an insurance salesman. From then on all the children said the same thing. The only ones who had real jobs were the Germans who owned bakeries, butcher shops or delicatessens. I really think most of the Germans came here with money or jewelry pinned to their underclothes because they weren't here five minutes when they owned a business. My friend Mary who was Italian, was saved by the bell when the day ended. Mary was frantic because she lived with her very old father and two sisters, one unmarried and the other married with a little boy. There wasn't any husband around. I told her I thought it was wrong for her to ask children such a question and I would go home and ask my father what to say. I told her to go home and ask her sister what she thought she should say. Poor Mary was a wreck, but I wasn't worried because I knew Daddy would take care of it for me.

He did tell me what to say and asked if I was afraid to stand up to her. I said I was not because I thought she was wrong. Many men were out of work including him and I was not going to say he was an insurance salesman. We got to school the next morning and I didn't have the chance to ask Mary if she was prepared, and I was worked up about her. She was called on first and she stood up and said her brother-in-law worked for the government. I sat across from her and we smiled at each other, as we were the only two in the class who knew he was in prison for armed robbery. When it came my turn I was a little nervous, but I stood up with my little heart beating and said , "My father said if you need to know what he does for a living, he will be happy to come in and speak with you." That stopped her cold. I guess she had overstepped her bounds. She said, "I think that is enough for today. Christina, why don't you pass out the reading books for our reading time?" That was it. I was still her pet and she never asked anyone else.

When I got home Daddy asked how I did and I told him I was a little scared, but it stopped her and he said I was a very brave girl. That meant more to me than anything. He had always told us to stand up for what we believed in. I guess that is why we are in Utah today because I was never afraid of the priests who were out of line.

SCHOOL LUNCH

I went to school at P.S. 3 on 157th Street between Melrose and Cortland Avenue in the Bronx. We had a building in the back of our school that was really old and wooden, and had a peaked roof. We would go in there for school lunch and this was supposed to help people feed their children at least one meal a day. Well you know how I feel about food and what a picky eater I am! I went inside and looked at the wooden picnic benches and I was ready to throw up! Our lunch was wheat bread and there was some kind of a spread on it, and there was a little container of milk, and the milk of course was starting to go sour. I don't like milk, I only like chocolate milk. The kids next door to us were always hungry, and they were very badly taken care of. Their father drank and eventually had to vacate the apartment for non-payment of rent. So we got to the lunch room and I couldn't eat what was being served. There was no way I could eat that day. I got together with the boy next door and I asked him, "Would you like to eat my lunch?" He said, "Oh Dena, I would love that—I'm hungry!" So we made an arrangement where we would sit at the picnic tables—which were horrible—facing each other, and he would hurry up and eat his lunch and then we would quickly switch the trays and of course the teachers were monitoring all of this, and after a couple of times we got caught. And that was the end of that!

MY WONDERFUL BED

I cannot explain to you our sleeping arrangements because they were too complicated for me to remember. We had three bedrooms and nine people, so my parents had to be pretty clever in arranging our sleeping quarters. I asked Peggy one time and she said she really didn't know. You just kept moving around.

When we were little we could sleep any place. Even have five children in one room. But, as we got a little older the three boys were set up in the big bedroom. Peggy, Mary and I slept in the smaller room all in one bed, and Bootsie I think had a cot in the living room.

When I got older I got my own bed, which was a Navy cot. I didn't mind that I didn't have a mattress, as the cot was very sturdy canvas. Besides, who knew any better? There was one problem though, the bed didn't fit into the space it was allotted. I had to maneuver it into the exact space so it would lay flat. I was not a very patient person and it nearly drove me crazy. It was so frustrating. I kicked it and banged it all over the room until finally it slipped into place. Meanwhile, no one thought to help me and I could hear Peggy and Mary laughing under the covers. This went on for quite a long time, sometimes twenty minutes or so. A strange thing happened though on the night of Uncle Larpse's funeral. I loved him and he was only about forty years old when he died of tuberculosis. He looked exactly like my father because he had lost so much weight. I thought of how someday I would have to stand and look at my father in his coffin and he would look just like my uncle. When I went home that night my bed slipped right into place and I got in peacefully, except I cried into my pillow all night.

Well, things change and along came World War II and Buddy joined the Navy. Even though I was so sad to see him go off to war, guess who got his bed? We changed again and the four girls got the big bedroom and the two boys got the small bedroom. Behind the French doors, which opened into the bedroom, was a space large enough for a cot and a small nightstand. When the door was opened into the bedroom it closed off half of my bedroom (so I called it). I always wanted my own bedroom and couldn't understand why I couldn't have one. I guess my mind was off in the clouds somewhere. I ironed at home to make some money for myself—now that I look back, the girls were pretty cheap, 5 cents for a blouse and 3 cents for a slip. But every payday they came home with a present for Bootsie and me, which was very appreciated.

With my ironing money I bought a two, deep drawer chest for my clothes. It was made of cardboard, but was nicely covered in blue wallpaper with little flowers in it. It was really very pretty and I found a small lamp for the top so I could read at night. I got a special book of Bible stories. We were not permitted to read the Bible in Catholic School- only the Catholic Doctrine in our catechism. The church felt it might teach us wrong doctrine-maybe like baby baptism or such. I was in heaven. I considered this my room and no one could go near it.

Well, as usual things always changed. The war ended, Buddy came home, and we were back to square one. I didn't mind though, because I was so happy he was safe while so many never came home at all, or came home emotionally ill or badly wounded.

Soon the older ones were starting to get married and I finally got my own room for a couple of years anyway. But then came the tuberculosis. While I was gone, Bootsie took over my room, and when I came home I booted her out and stayed there for six months until I got married. There I was sharing a room again. Now I pray I never have my own room again.

RELEASED TIME FROM SCHOOL
FOR RELIGIOUS INSTRUCTION

Since we went to public school we were released from class one hour early one day a week, so we would be prepared to make our First Holy Communion and then our Confirmation. This took four years to accomplish. Two nuns would come to our school to pick us up and take us to St. Peter and Paul's School. One would stand at the front of the line and one at the back. We were marched in a line two by two and were not permitted to speak to anyone. The first nun would blow her whistle when she was ready to cross the street and the second nun would then blow hers so we could proceed. This went on for about four blocks. Those nuns sure loved their whistles and we were sick to death of them. They kept them hidden in the pleats of their long skirts. I think it gave them some power over us. They were mean and loved to catch you doing something wrong. We were terrified of them. One day as we got to the stairs of the school my friend Doris whispered to me that she would meet me outside after release time. Sister Noella, the school principal grabbed her arm and twisted it behind Doris's back. Doris was in pain and started crying. Sister Noella was not my favorite person after that.

We also had to attend the 9 o'clock mass on Sunday. We were then marched over to the school for one more hour of instruction. After two years we had to appear in front of Sister Noella while she threw questions at us to be sure we were properly indoctrinated. We were never allowed to read the Bible in case it should not be interpreted the way the Catholic Church felt it should be.

My turn came to be tested. All the nuns had very large sleeves and kept their arms tucked in each one. I always thought that if we gave a wrong answer out would come a ruler from the one of the sleeves. They thought nothing of hitting us with rulers. In our class at public school Bootsie and I had a problem with the boys behind us dipping the ends of our braids in the ink well, we would have blue tips on our braids. Bootsie was worse off because she was so blonde. I had dark hair. That day I had blue braids and I had to go before Sister Noelle. I knew this would make her crazy so I put my hair behind my back so she wouldn't see them. I was so happy when the test was over and I had passed without any bodily injury. I had planned on quickly moving my braids before I left her, but in my relief of having passed I forgot the braids, and I just started to walk away. Suddenly I hear "CHRISTINA, WHY ARE YOUR BRAIDS BLUE?" I had to stand there while she carried on about boys touching my hair, etc. I just kept saying, "Yes, Sister, yes, Sister." All the while I was thinking she was just jealous because I was sure no boy ever touched her hair. Besides I had these thick Irish braids and she didn't have any hair at all. For the next two years until Confirmation exams I kept my braids pinned on top of my head so no one could get near them on Religious Instruction day.

GOING TO CONFESSION

Before you could make your Communion you had to go to your first confession. The priests then wanted you to go every week after that. We were little children so what sins could we possibly have.

We went on Saturday evening and stood on line with the other children until it was our turn to enter the dreaded box. The priest then heard our confession and gave us our penance to say afterward. Everyone lined up on Monsignor McCarthy's confessional because he had such a thick Irish brogue you couldn't tell what he was saying. So if he was upset with you it didn't matter. However, we had a monster priest who would have no one on his line so he would come out and take some children off the other line. That was like the worst thing that could happen to you.

One sin you never wanted to confess would be if you missed mass on Sunday. That was worse that committing murder. You would be read the riot act and told you would burn in the fires of hell if you didn't attend to your duty and get yourself to mass. You would also have a penance that would keep you in the church half the night.

The real problem was that we didn't have any sins to confess. So as any smart child would do we would make up sins. You would say that you had a fight with your brother or that you told a lie; whatever you could think of. The one you never said was that you talked back to your mother. Any priest worth his salt living in that neighborhood would know you would be in the hospital getting "the last rites of the church" if you ever did that. Of course talking back to your father wasn't even a consideration.

One day in Sunday school the nun made an oval on the board and filled it in completely with chalk until it was completely white. This was our pure soul, before we goofed up and started messing it up. She would take her thumb and rub some calk on it for each sin we committed and soon it was all black. I remember how much I wanted that pure should and would go to confession every Saturday and Communion every Sunday.

When confession was completed I would go to kneel at the altar and say my penance and then leave the church with the most glorious feeling. I was as pure as the driven snow and God was so happy with me. It never occurred to me that I had just lied in the confessional.

I remember a few times the priest saying "Now child do you ever have any impure thoughts?" "WHAT"S THAT?" I had no idea what that was all about, but it sure sounded like a "NO FATHER" to me. Knowing what we know now about the priests I wonder if he was just hoping to get a good little story for his anxious ears. We were only about six to ten years old.

MORNINGS

Getting seven children off to school in the morning was not an easy task, especially with only one bathroom. Daddy was a perfectionist and was always very organized. He decided we could each have 15 minutes in the bathroom in the morning. Mary liked to get up early so she was first one to get up at 6:00 am. I was the last. One parent would make the breakfast, the other lunches. The lunch bags would all be lined up on the kitchen cupboard for us to grab on our way out. First Daddy had to check everyone over and one morning Jimmy was on his way, books under his arm, lunch bag in his fist and his tie around his neck and no shirt!

One time they decided to surprise us with a special lunch. Daddy made a whole bunch of Ritz crackers with peanut butter and jelly. There was a cracker on the bottom, then peanut butter and jelly with a cracker on top. He must have made a hundred of them. At times he missed and the jelly would flop on the table which was very upsetting to him because he had no patience. We were at the table choking with laughter on our "cruel gruel." After school Jimmy came home all upset saying that someone had stolen his "sammitch" and left him only dessert.

I was never a morning person and it was difficult to get me up for school. My father used to greet me each morning saying "good morning merry sunshine." It was Buddy's job to get me to school on time. He must have graduated early from the eighth grade. It seems he was on his way to Stuyvesant High School. He couldn't be late and I was so slow. I had a nice winter coat with a big fur collar. I would stick my chin inside my collar and he would pick me up by the back of the collar and off we would go the three blocks to PS3 with my little legs kicking in the air.

During the week we always had oatmeal for breakfast. My father made it every morning and Mary, sarcastic even then, called it "cruel gruel" (never to his face of course.) On Sunday mornings we had a treat--buns from the German bakery. The one who went got "first pick." Soon you would hear throughout the apartment "I get second pick, "I get third" and so on. The last one got no pick at all, but the last bun left and as a consolation the crumbs at the bottom of the bag.

EASTER

I seem to remember that we always had new clothes on Easter Sunday. Mom would stay up all night sewing our dresses. In the morning we would have to pass Daddy's inspection. He was very proud of his brood. We would then go to Mass and then off to show the relatives our finery. We would visit Aunt Mary, Uncle Eddie and Uncle Tommy – my father's sister and brothers. When you visited Uncles Eddie and Tommy you always got one dollar each. Uncle Tommy was a building inspector and Uncle Eddie was a wire lather. Every Easter morning there would be seven beautiful Easter baskets lined up on the dining room buffet filled with candy.

MOTHER'S DAY

When I was a little girl I would always run around to 159th Street where there was a huge lilac bush at the front of a nice private house. My mother loved lilacs, so after church I would sneak around the street with my scissors in my pocket and hack away until I had a huge bouquet. No one ever came out to yell at me, so I thought it was probably sort of like the peach tree, it was there, no one complained, so why waste it. I don't remember if she ever asked me where they came from. Maybe Mama had a deal for the flowers with the owner. She may have received a great meal from Mama and Mama's little darling wasn't stealing. I am sure Daddy followed me one day and spoke to the lady. He was a real schemer.

One time I saved all my pennies from my candy money for ten days and was determined to get something special for Mama. That was quite a bit of money for a child back then, but I was determined to get just the right thing. I didn't know what it was so I had to really hunt through the stores. On Saturday I went down to the Dry Goods store on Melrose Ave. and 158th Street. These were really big stores and carried everything but food and furniture. It took quite a while, but nothing impressed me. I then went down three blocks to Third Avenue and 159th Street to another Dry Goods store and checked the whole thing out and then suddenly way in the back, there it was, a perfect little tea pot just for Mama! I was so happy because Mama always made big pots of tea for everyone and I wanted something just for her if she wanted to make just one pot for herself in the afternoons when we were in school.

She loved it and used it all the time. The top got broken, but she kept it on a shelf in the kitchen and I have it now on a shelf in my dining room. I hope one of my children will keep it also.

It was quite an adventure for me because I was only about seven years old and I was running all over the Bronx neighborhoods all by myself.

Mama used to read tea leaves for us. Her grandmother taught her and we thought is was exciting. One night when I was about seventeen, I asked her to read mine and she said:

There is a baseball player in there.

Oh Mama, come on – stop teasing me. What do you really see?

I see a baseball player.

Give me that – let me see! He was standing exactly the way Huey always held his bat. If it was possible, I would still have those tea leaves, but the real player was much better. Everyone had a good laugh at me, but I had the last laugh!

FATHER'S DAY

Usually on Father's Day most men would receive the usual socks, handkerchiefs, or a new Sunday shirt because people didn't have much money to buy anything large or expensive. No matter what Daddy got he would make a big fuss like he didn't get the same thing last year and the year before that. As we got older and all had enough money to chip in we would buy him a pack of Chesterfield Cigarettes. They were his favorite brand, but were a little more expensive than the others.

Usually he would send us for a pack of Bull Durham Tobacco. It came in a package which was pulled up tight to the top and pulled closed tight with string. On the side was a packet of thin papers. He would then take one paper, fill it with the tobacco and lick the ends then make a cigarette. I used to watch this because it wasn't easy to do.

In our kitchen we had a table and two chairs. Mama always sat on one side near the window and Daddy sat on the side near the stove. I can see him now rolling up the tobacco. Since we didn't have matches, he would bend over and light his cigarette in the fire. I was always nervous he might get burned.

It was always a great day when we would hand him his pack of Chesterfields. Sometimes we would save our babysitting money and surprise him with one when we got home from school.

What surprises me is that we were little children and could go into the store and buy beer and cigarettes without any problem.

One year for a special gift we gave him a huge teacup with the word "Daddy" written on it. He made such a fuss about how much he loved it. It held about 3 cups of tea. When you made tea for him in it, you had to take cold water from the tap and boil it in the kettle, and then take that and pour it into the empty teacup (no teabags in the cup) as the purpose of this was just to heat the cup. While the cup was getting warm, you had to dump all of the water out of the tea kettle and fill it back up with cold water. When it began to whistle, you poured the hot water out of the now warm teacup, added three teabags and then filled it up with the new boiling water. If you cheated and skipped a step he knew it right away and then you had to start all over again!

ST. PATRICK'S DAY

Of course, we always had corned beef and cabbage on St. Patrick's Day. There was always a bit of beer or Irish Whiskey on hand too. Maldacher's Saloon would sponsor a big bash at the Embassy Ballroom which was around the corner from us. Everyone in the neighborhood would go and as you can imagine there was always plenty of good refreshment to drink. Irish music was played all night and we would sing all the old Irish songs. I always did the Irish Jig with Daddy, who could just about stand up by the end of the evening. He must have been in his later fifties at that time. It was absolutely wonderful.

HALLOWEEN

Holidays were always looked forward to. Halloween was my parents' wedding anniversary. They were married in 1920. We had a party every year. Trick or treat didn't begin until the late 1950's so it was unusual for people to have a special party. We had a decoration that looked like a hula skirt. It was black and orange and was hung around the ceiling light which gave the room an orange glow. We also had a pumpkin with a candle in it that we hung in the French doorway. One year it caught the wood frame on fire and my poor father was so upset. He was so afraid of fire we thought he must have seen some terrible ones in the old tenements. We had little orange and black candy cups with our names on them and we kept them from year to year. Then we would fill a big pan of water and dunk for apples. Every year someone would say to Daddy, "You have been married a long time now, so don't you think you should take the Halloween mask off?" Every year Daddy laughed and would tell us how they met.

THANKSGIVING

Thanksgiving was always a big feast. We would have turkey with all the trimmings. My mother always made her wonderful stuffing. I still have the chopping bowl and chopper that was used to prepare the celery, onions, mushrooms, and sausage. Daddy would put a towel on the windowsill to keep down the noise and seemed to be chopping all day. You were never allowed in the kitchen while all this activity was taking place, but the smells were heavenly. On the buffet were big bowls of mixed nuts, oranges and apples. We had cut up celery, pickles and olives. My parents ate at the big table with us on all holidays. The other days they would feed us then have a quiet meal in the kitchen. I don't know where the money came from for the bounty, but I suspected Uncle Tommy had something to do with it. My father's family didn't always agree with each other, but they always took care of one another. If we somehow had extra, Aunt Nellie, who was divorced with five little girls, always got some.

WINTERTIME

Buddy loved to ice-skate. The YMCA was one block away from our house and had an outdoor rink with a big fence around it. I don't know where he got the skates or the money from, but he went often with his friends. Sometimes Peggy and Mary would go too. It wasn't as much fun for Peggy, she had a difficult time because her ankles always caved inward. Somehow he got me some little two runner skates and I went a few times. We younger ones would mostly watch through the fence. The word would get out that Buddy was skating and we would all run to watch. It was so festive with the music, the spotlights and everyone skating round and round. I can see it even now.

One year Buddy made a pair of skis. In order to bend the tips he set them in a bucket of hot water in the bathtub. We were about ready to murder him because we could not take a bath until his project was finished. He would not allow us to remove the skis and we were wild. Looking back now, I wonder how we let him get away with that.

CHRISTMAS

On Christmas Eve my mother would take all seven of us to buy the tree. We would all stand there in the tree lot looking up at the biggest tree they had. The tree man couldn't charge too much to such a lovely lady with all those little urchins. All seven of us would carry the tree home. We would be in a row, Peggy first (at the bottom which was the heaviest) on down to Bootsie. We would laugh and sing all the way home. The tree was always trimmed after dinner and it was always the most beautiful in the neighborhood. My mother had a way of doing everything just right and it truly was beautiful. Then we would sit around the radio with Daddy and listen to Lionel Barrymore play Scrooge. When Tiny Tim said, "God bless us, every one" Daddy would always have to wipe the tears from his eyes. Then we would hang up our stockings, eagerly anticipating the goodies we would find in them the next morning. We all wanted Mary's stockings because she had the longest legs!

In the morning we would find lots of toys and stockings filled with nuts, candy, and an orange and an apple. I don't remember what we ate on Christmas Day in the earlier years, but we had prime rib in the later years when everyone started working.

One year I got a beautiful doll house and Buddy, Peggy, and Mary stayed up almost all night playing with it. They made it into Aunt Mary's apartment which apparently had many visitors over the years. They had chairs pushed together to make beds for all the company. They also thought it would be hilarious to put the bathroom in the entryway of the doll house. As soon as you walked in the front door you were greeted by the toilet!!

Every year Mama got at least one bottle of Blue Waltz perfume for Christmas. This luxury item was purchased at Woolworth's, the local five and ten. The cost of Blue Waltz was 10 cents for a small bottle, and as children we thought we were buying her Chanel No. 5. In later years I wondered what Mama did with all the Blue Waltz perfume.

As we got older we all bought presents for each other. Peggy and Mary had the job of wrapping. They would get out a bottle of wine and get started. They would soon be writing tags out, "To Jimmy from Eddie, To Eddie from Jimmy, To Buddy from Eddie, and To Buddy from Buddy." Whoops! That didn't sound right! So they would have a good old time. One year we had 78 presents all over the piano and under the tree. That year we bought Daddy a watch and wrapped it up in a tea bag box so he would not guess what he was getting. He made such a big fuss about it, all day he wore his sleeve rolled up and asked if we needed to know the time.

We had a small tree one year only. The year the war was over the tree sellers were charging enormous amounts for the big trees. The servicemen were coming home with mustering out pay for their first Christmas since the war. That year my parents went to get the tree and came home with a small one. We could not believe our eyes and thought they were just teasing us. Then Daddy told us how outraged he was that the trees were so very high priced and the servicemen were being taken advantage of. He was upset and would not buy a big tree. That year we were all proud of our little tree.

GINGERBREAD COOKIES

One Christmas, Peggy, Buddy and Mary decided they would make some Gingerbread cookies for all of us. I don't know how my mother put up with all this nonsense. She had a very small kitchen and had to cook for nine people. But, she seemed to really enjoy all the activity.

They decided that they would speak only in German. Not one word of English could be used. They were very busy mixing the dough, adding all the spices and cutting out the little men. Then they had to cut them out and put them on cookie sheets and into the oven. When the cookies cooled they decorated them with icing and they really were cute. They were having a wonderful time.

I think though that they were paying more attention to their German conversation than to the ingredients they were using as the little men came out as hard as a rock. There wasn't any way they could be eaten so we drilled holes in the top of their heads, strung red ribbon through the holes and hung them on the tree. They were even heavy for the tree and made the branches bend down a bit. We all teased them for quite a time after that. It was really fun to watch the baking and listen to the German. I remember all the fun they had that day.

NEW YEAR'S EVE

One New Year's Eve after the war, but before anyone was married, Mary went to a big party with Victor Winter or possibly Dan O'Conner, who lived in our same building, (I can't remember which boy it was), at the local YMCA which was just one block away from us. Peggy wasn't very happy, as Mary really got dressed up and Peggy did not like not having a date. She and I were home alone while everyone else was at some celebration. When Mary came home Peggy asked her if she had a nice time. The conversation went as follows:

Peggy: Did you have a nice time?

Mary: Well, I was kind of sad and didn't really enjoy myself.

Peggy: What are you talking about? Here poor Dena and I were stuck alone and you got all dressed up and went out on a date.

Mary: Well, it was a blind band.

Dena: A BLIND BAND? What's that? I never heard of such a thing.

Mary: They were blind. They could not see. When they came in and out of the room they had to hold on to the shoulder in front of them and had to slide their feet so they wouldn't fall. It really put a damper on the evening.

Dena: Why didn't you leave?

Mary: I felt it would be insulting and I didn't want to hurt their feelings.

Dena: How would they know you left when they couldn't see? (Not one of my better moments.)

Peggy: At least they had a job. If everyone left they wouldn't have a job and what would they do to make a living?

The conversation ended there, except I was annoyed that Peggy said I was poor Dena who didn't have a date or a party to go to. I didn't date and didn't want to go to a party, as I knew Huey wouldn't be there. Instead I stayed home with Peggy listening to hours of crazy operas. I didn't care for them, but put up with their screeching and yelling in another language. Everyone was stabbing themselves, or someone was crying over the death of someone dying from tuberculosis. She had to take advantage of Daddy being out of the house because he would not put up with them at all. What a headache.

I told them we should have all gone to Maldacher's where half the block would be and probably most of our family, and we would have all had a great time.

Several years ago we visited Peggy and she had some of our friends from the old neighborhood for dinner. Of course we spent the whole evening reminiscing about all the old times we had on 160th Street. She told the story of Mary's party and Larry, with out a moment's hesitation asked. "What did they play? I only have eyes for you?" Green Eyes and smoke gets in your eyes and who cares. We could not stop laughing because it was so spontaneous.

OUR SHOES

I don't remember having a new pair of shoes during the 1930's or the early 1940's. During the Depression the main concern was to pay the rent and feed the family. Anything else was a luxury to be enjoyed on rare occasions. By the time the war was in its early years my older sisters were working while going to school at night to get a college education. Buddy joined the Navy and sent home an allotment of money, which was matched by the government, so things were improving at home. Still money was tight for a family of nine so that even new shoes were rare.

During the Depression we all wore hand me down clothes, but the shoes were always the worst. I don't know who they started with. Perhaps a cousin who had outgrown them and then passed them off to somebody else. If the pair you were assigned was too large we then stuffed the toes with newspaper until they fit. Most of the soles were pretty well worn so you didn't have them very long before you had a hole in the sole. We then cut out a piece of cardboard to fit the inside of the shoe and off we went. Of course that wouldn't last very long and you would keep using the cardboard until the hole was so big it would get through to your socks and burn the bottom of your foot. The next step was to go to the dry goods store on Melrose Avenue to buy a package that contained your size sole and some awful smelling glue. Mama would paint the sole with the glue and then apply the rubber sole until it stuck. This worked great. You almost felt like you had new shoes. It also lasted a few weeks and then the front part of the sole began to loosen and you walked with it flopping up and down. We were lucky we didn't trip and fall because they were awkward once the glue loosened. The laces were also a problem. Because they were so old , they would of course break, so we fixed this by making knots in them. Then the challenge became how to get the laces with all those knots in them through the eyelets. Many days were spent tugging knots through holes.

The next step would be to take the shoes to the shoe repair man, who had a store on Melrose Avenue, and have him put on a new sole. This was a last resort as it cost money we didn't have, and the shoes were not worth the money so we just moved on to the next hand me down shoes. It really wasn't too traumatic because most of the children in the neighborhood were in the same situation. They were flopping around in their shoes too. Actually we would have a good laugh deciding who was flopping more.

The shoe man was Italian. I only tell you this because I want you to know how diverse our neighborhood was and how most of the people had the same trades as their own kind. I had all kinds of friends and I loved it. They were all so different because many were first generation children and so you cold learn a lot about their culture. The Italian children all wore a string around their necks attached to a piece of garlic. The old people insisted this would keep them healthy. Actually it did! This could have been mainly because no one wanted to get near them so they didn't get anyone's germs.

The shoe man also had a business in his store of blocking men's hats. They all wore fedoras which had to keep their shape or they looked wilted. One time I went to pick up my father's hat. It was the first time I had been in the shop. I loved the smell of the leather and watched the shoe man put the soles on the shoes and hammer nails, which he held in his mouth, into the soles and then he trimmed them with a sharp knife. I was fascinated by all this activity and hated to leave. He must have noticed my interest because he took the time to explain what he was doing.

HAND ME DOWN CLOTHES

If we had hand me down shoes, surely we would have hand me down clothes. The dresses and skirts were not too bad because Mama was the best seamstress ever. Whenever she could get a piece of cloth on sale she would measure us and then make her own pattern from the daily newspaper. They were somewhat plain as she couldn't afford to pay for numerous trimmings, however they were also pretty.

Mama made all of our Easter, Communion and Confirmation clothes, and they were beautiful. She had all the trimmings she felt were necessary and was very happy with the result. I don't know where the money came from, but my brothers even had nice suits. These religious holy days were very important to her.

The home relief gave us some clothes at school time. Each of the girls got two new dresses which weren't too bad, but all the kids in the neighborhood had the same dresses. When Mama made us something new it was a real treat.

The boys received two pairs each of blue corduroy knickers and shirts to start school. They may have gotten a tie for assembly also. All the boys would swish, swish all around the halls of school. In the winter my younger sister and I would use them as snow pants because they were longer on us and kept us warm.

We would shop in the dry goods store for such things as horrible heavy cotton stockings which were very ugly but warm. The little girls would wear a vest with long straps on them with a clip at the end to keep the stockings up. You would be proud to be grown up enough to get a real garter belt and silk stockings. You would tell the owner how long your legs were and she would measure the stockings to fit you. No pantyhose back then.

I babysat for a German lady and one Christmas she gave me two beautiful dresses. I could hardly believe my eyes when I opened the box. One was very pretty, but the other was magnificent. It was a black and red plaid and had a big white collar with lace trim and appliquéd roses on the shoulders and front. I felt like a queen in that dress and thank her now for how happy she made me.

The real problem with hand me downs were the coats. They never fit and came from who knows in the family. You just kept passing them around the family. Of course they were not pretty. They were too short or too long and they always had holes in the pockets because the pockets were made of cheap material and after so much wear they would just tear to pieces.

One awful day in the second grade, we were all ready to be dismissed and I could not find my mittens. Everyone had gone home and I was driving the teacher crazy because I was crying so hard. I told her we had just bought them the night before and I could not go home without them. I looked through every desk and every closet getting more upset with every failure. The teacher asked me where I got them I told her the dry good's store on Melrose Avenue. She wanted to know how much they cost and I said, "TEN CENTS." She probably wanted to kill me for tearing the place apart and keeping her all that time. She gave me the ten cents and told me to go back and get another pair and she would be happy to pay for them. I happily went home with my mittens and when I walked in the door Mama asked me what was in the hem of my coat. You got it – my mittens had fallen through the hole in my pocket. Now I was really in a mess because if Daddy knew I took money from the teacher he would have a fit. So I dropped the whole mess on Mama and as usual she told me not to worry and she sent a nice note to the teacher the next day enclosing a dime. Daddy didn't find out which was surprising as he was up on everything. Sometimes life could be rough for a little seven year old. But, I got over the embarrassment and life went on as usual.

DADDY'S SOUP

Daddy liked to make soup and would never throw away any kind of bone that had one piece of meat on it. This was a good way to fill up seven children along with Mama's home made bread.

First you headed to Tony's for 25 cents worth of soup greens. He had a special size brown bag for this and knew exactly how much of the greens to put in the bag. He put in parsley, potatoes, onion, tomatoes, leeks and whatever. He marked it down and then you headed to the Butcher Shop for the soup meat. That was marked down also. You had to have a pretty thick skin to grow up in the Bronx during the Depression.

Daddy was then ready to make his vegetable soup which he was very proud of because it was hearty and good for us. I was a very picky eater and hated the soup, but he always made me something different like eggs. We never had to eat food we didn't like.

One evening we were all set for our supper (dinner was called supper back then) when Daddy suddenly got all upset in the kitchen. We all crowded into the kitchen to see what excitement might be going on. Daddy could not find his favorite pot holder which he probably had since he got married. We all searched the kitchen for it, but it was no where to be found. He said "don't worry about it. It will turn up." Well it certainly did. As he was scooping out the last of the soup out came the dirty, greasy potholder. Everyone agreed it was the best soup they ever had. From then on Daddy's vegetable soup was called "potholder soup." Kind of fun to get one up on Daddy as he knew every move we made. We couldn't get away with anything.

THE LIBRARY

Poor Peggy, since she was the eldest every time she went somewhere she had to drag one of the little ones along. Because she was such a good student she did a lot of her research at the library. I thought the library was fascinating. It was at the end of a lovely street which had all private homes and trees all the way up to the corner of the library. On the opposite side of the street were beautiful apartment houses that had big courts in the center with about eight apartments surrounding the court. Interestingly after Huey and I were married we got a lovely apartment on a street very close. It also had a court surrounded by the apartments. This is where I got the apartment for Peggy. She made a lot of good friends (all Irish Catholic) while I spent my spare time at Mama's, which was about four blocks away. While I was at Mama's, Huey was still playing stick ball.

When you entered the library's double doors you went up a wide flight of stairs which led into the main section. Up another flight was the children's library, but Peggy never let me up there because she was afraid I might wander off and get lost. One time as we were walking, she had me in the carriage and Eddie and Jimmy on each side holding on the handle. When she crossed the street she realized Jimmy was gone. She was hysterical and traced her route back to where they had come from. How could she lose our little Jimmy? How could she go home and tell our parents Jimmy was gone? She was crying, Eddie was crying. It was horrible. Then she saw some people standing around a piece of the curb, and sure enough, there was Jimmy crying because he was lost. Peggy was always very petite like Mama and Jimmy was always a big, strong Irish boy. It must have been quite a sight because they were built so differently. She was kissing and hugging him like mad. It's a good thing Eddie didn't wander off while all this commotion was going on.

When we got to the library she plopped me down in a place they had for children whose caretakers needed time to find their books. The lower shelf was all children's books and I found one that I loved, "The Sunflower Sisters." I opened it up and the first page had two sisters with beautiful pure white sunflower hats. The illustrations were so pretty. The sisters were always working hard in the house and in the garden. I wanted to see their faces, but low and behold I went through the whole book and never saw a face. I finally went to the next book and still no face. Finally I went through the whole set and no one had a face. I would quickly turn a page thinking maybe I would catch them when they weren't looking. I was so frustrated I went up to the librarian, scary as it was as she seemed very stern to me, and asked her, "Where are the girl's faces? She attempted to explain to me that the importance of the book was the bonnets and not the girls, but I was having none of that. So I went to Peggy and told her the librarian didn't understand the books and I wanted to know where the faces were. I bet Peggy was happy she brought me along. While she was busy studying I was annoying everyone about faces. Every time we went I looked through the books especially if there was a new one. Surely they would have a face in that one. Anyway, I finally gave up and moved on to more sensible books.

I was very interested in the librarian. She looked very official and in control of everything. Too bad she didn't know anything about books!! She had a rack with wheels on it filled with books which she rolled around putting books away. I wondered how she knew where they went. Then Peggy checked out and she had a library card. The librarian had a funny looking stamp on her pencil and she turned it over and stamped the book and then Peggy's card. Of course I questioned Peggy all about these interesting things all the way home. She explained very patiently. I told her the next time we came I was going to get my own card. Then she had to tell me I was too young to have a library card, but if I wanted to take out a book I could put it on her card. I'm surprised she ever took me back, but she never went without me. I didn't check out any books because I couldn't even read.

In grade and high school I went there often to do my homework and research projects for school.

I liked school projects, so I was always volunteering for one. One time it was on safety. I didn't think I wanted to give Daddy's street smarts. I wanted something that would really stand out. I thought about it and suddenly realized the Police Station should have posters and material on safety. So away I went into the station and talked to a policeman, told him what I wanted, and asked, "Could you help me?" He said, "Come back in a few days and I will have great posters for you." Well they came in early so he decided to deliver them to our home. I hadn't mentioned it to anyone. The policeman rang the bell. Poor Daddy answered and the man asked if a Christina Lynch lived there. Poor Daddy thought I was dead. He asked what happened to me. Was I alive or in the hospital? He was told that he was just there to deliver some posters and material I requested for school. When I got home Daddy wanted to know why I hadn't told anyone. He couldn't believe I marched right into the police station and got what I went for. Usually the police never came to your house unless he had very bad news.

I had beautiful large posters all over the blackboard. I was so proud. The teacher asked where I found them and I told her the Police Station. She looked at me a little strangely. Well, I got an A+ on my project and we almost lost poor Daddy.

PEGGY'S 8TH GRADE GRADUATION

The year was 1937 and money was tight. However, money wasn't of importance as this was the first child graduating and there was a good chance Peggy was going to receive one of the three medals given to the best student.

I was only five years old but remember the day pretty well because it was such a wonderful day for Daddy. He didn't get through the 2nd grade but taught himself to read and write and was determined every one of his children would get an education. The day we started 1st grade and all the way through school we were told in no uncertain terms that we had to graduate from high school. If we wanted to go on to college that would be wonderful, but high school was mandatory.

Peggy made her dress as that was the 8th grade sewing project. My mother took Peggy to the beauty parlor (that was what we called the hairdresser) for the latest style, which was "The Marcel" and Peggy hated it and was very annoyed. My mother made the bows for her hair and Peggy wore my mother's pearl necklace. In later years we called her "Jewels" because she always wore jewelry.

They then went to Woolworths on Third Avenue to have her picture taken. We didn't have color film at the time so the store hired someone to paint the picture by hand with water colors. Her corsage probably came from our uncle Larpse.

As young as I was I can remember how proud Daddy was and when Peggy walked on the stage to receive the "Gold Medal" the highest medal of achievement, Daddy was ecstatic. He knew this child was going on to college!

I think Buddy and Mary each received medals too when they graduated.

THE GERMAN DINNER PARTY

One evening Buddy, Peggy, and Mary decided to have a German dinner, and everyone had to speak German. In fact, you could not speak at the table unless it was in German. They invited all of their German speaking friends and served German potato pancakes, and applesauce. They had a very memorable time. We four younger ones were not permitted to say a word. I did work for a German lady babysitting for her and I understood a lot of their conversations.

RUSHING THE GROWLER

On Sundays in the summer while my parents were making dinner, Daddy would get down the beer can, put on his straw hat and head to the German Beer Garden up the street. The beer can was called a growler. It was a small tin can with a long handle and was used to carry beer from the saloon. This was called "Rushing the Growler." If Daddy went by himself he could go in the front door of the bar, but if we went with him he would go to the side door which had a sign "Ladies Welcome" on it. When you opened the door a bell attached to the top of the door would ring as you entered the "back room" as it was called. There were tablecloths and baskets of the most delicious pretzels. Mr. Maldacher would step from behind the bar in his long white apron and step down the two steps to the back room, make a big fuss over the children, all the while smiling through his big handlebar mustache. He would give us some pretzels and take the growler. You could peek around the corner to look into the forbidden bar room and see the beautiful shiny bar with its glistening brass rail while Mr. Maldacher filled the can from the tap. Sometimes on the way home Daddy would let us have a sip of the suds on the top.

If the growler made too many trips to Maldacher's and Daddy was sentimental, Mary and I would be called on to do our little song and dance routine for them. We thought we were stars headed for Broadway. We danced and sang our songs, "You must have been a beautiful baby" and "Little old lady time for tea." Our finale would be a tap dance with Daddy to "East Side West Side." The evening would end with Daddy singing to Mama "If You Were The Only Girl in the World" and "If I Had My Way."

The growler always made trips on Mother's Day and I can remember that my father (as well as the other men in the neighborhood) wore black arm bands on their long sleeved shirts. This was in memory of their deceased mothers. I was very moved by this show of love and respect for mothers. Only the men wore these bands. When I would iron my father's handkerchiefs and put them in his dresser drawer next to where he had the black band, I used to pick it up and hold it in my hands. As I held it I would wonder about my grandmother, and what she was like. I wished that I could talk to her and ask her questions, and listen to the sound of her voice. Some traditions should never go away. I wish I would have saved the band and the growler.

THE PAINTERS

After we moved into our apartment the landlord sent three big German painters to paint the apartment, which was very nice except they did the whole five rooms in two days. Everything was painted white with huge brushes, no rollers then! We were afraid to stand next to the wall or we would get painted right over. They didn't waste one minute. I do not know how my parents did it. The paint smelled terrible and was probably filled with lead. The first day, as I remember it, they painted the bathroom, kitchen and hallway. Everything had to be removed from those rooms. I don't know what they could have fed us, as we certainly didn't have any take out places. And they had nowhere to cook or put pots. I imagine we all got bologna sandwiches. The second day they painted the three bedrooms. I don't even remember where we slept, but then that was nothing new. We were always moving beds around to suit one group or another. I remember everything we owned piled on top of our old round table. It was big and could really hold a lot. Poor Peggy who was a maniac student was sitting on top of the pile almost to the ceiling crying her eyes out because she wouldn't get her homework done. I am laughing now because I can still see her. I wish I had a picture of it. We little ones were under the table playing cards and games whispering to each other, "NO HOMEWORK, NO HOMEWORK TONIGHT." It was almost like a horror movie – all these big men running around with paint and us trying to stay out of their way. They were known in the neighborhood as, "The Schmearers."

We endured this twice. One day the landlord announced "the painters" were coming and my mother said we would paint our own apartment in the future. We had a little money coming in and she would paint one room at a time and in a color she liked. We were so happy because when it was announced "the painters" were coming the whole building would be moaning.

MAMA COMES DOWN WITH SPINAL MENINGITIS

Oh what heartbreak for all of us because the doctor said nothing could save her. In the very early part of the war Jimmy got meningitis, but he was a big strapping boy and Mama was so little and much older.

Jimmy got very sick and Daddy called the doctor and he came to the house. What did I just say – The doctor made house calls? He thought that Jimmy had the flu which at that time they called "The Grippe." The symptoms were all the same, except near the ends his neck and eyes hurt terribly. Daddy ran down to the Police Station to call an ambulance. We didn't have a phone and Daddy felt the ambulance would arrive much sooner if the call came from there. They came and my parents went with him. They discovered he had meningitis and he was gravely ill. We were all crying. How could we lose our beloved brother? We were all broken hearted until he got better and came home.

Then about two years later Mama got very sick. The doctor came again. Did I just say that again? The doctor thought she had "The Grippe", but Daddy was worried. Two days later she complained of her eyes hurting. He kept me home from school so he could leave her while he ran to get an ambulance. He wouldn't let me go in her room because he was sure she would be contagious. I wanted so badly to be with her and comfort her, but I knew Daddy was very frightened. I saw them take her out in the ambulance. She was so little all I could see was her face and it was all yellow. I can still see her and can hardly get through this part of my story. I wanted so badly to go with them because Daddy needed comforting now. He was so nervous.

I went into my little wonderful bed and got on my knees and prayed my heart out. I must have been there at least three hours. I begged God to save our mother. Daddy would surely die without her. There was no question about that in my mind. What could we do without Mama? I could barely stand the pain of it. Finally I told God I was going to pray right there if it took forever. All of a sudden I got this warm peaceful feeling come over me and I knew she would live.

Daddy came home then and sat in his usual chair and started sobbing. He told me my mother was going to die and he had to come home to tell the children. The Red Cross had already sent for Buddy. I told him our mother would not die and he asked me not to make it any more difficult for he still had to tell the other children and he didn't know how he could bring himself to do it. I went into his drawer and brought out another handkerchief for him and told him not to cry anymore because I knew she would live. He wanted to know how I could be sure when the doctors said it was impossible to save her. Except for one doctor who said to Peggy while I was praying that he would do everything in his power to save her. I told him that God told me. Many times later he told me how he wondered how the doctor should say it would be over soon and his little girl looks like an angel telling me she would live.

Mama came home two weeks later. I ran in the door after school and ran into her arms so fast I almost knocked her over. What a wonderful reunion we all had and how I thanked God for this blessing in our lives.

THE DOCTOR'S OFFICE

I am so amazed at the advances made in the medical profession in my lifetime. I am so grateful that I was here to see how it became such a huge industry that was capable of saving so many lives and helping the sick. The machines they have now (which I hate) are unbelievable. The technology is amazing. I worked in the billing department of what now looks like a medical center. They have grown so they can do almost everything right there. I would love to be capable of being a part of all the excitement and all the different departments, but my health is poor and I am going on eighty years of age and I can remember my life stories, but can't keep track of anything else. I had a stomach scope and colonoscopy today and the doctor asked how old I am and I had to think a minute. Then I told him I was 79 years old and he said I was a very young 79 year old--yeah right-- I felt like 100 when we were finished. Then the anesthesia didn't work and he went ahead anyway. It was so painful I will never do it again and a Hex on the doc. I really hoped I could get through this life without being tortured by an Arab!

When we were children Daddy had a family doctor. He saw him a lot because of his stomach but usually at his office or the hospital. Peggy said I got all his gifts – TB, stomach problems they could never diagnose except for an ulcer (which I will have soon if I don't calm my stomach down). He couldn't drive a car and neither can I. I ace the written tests, but when I get behind the wheel I freeze. He couldn't put a nail in the wall without wrecking the wall and guess who can't do the same? Mama did everything and so does Huey. Huey would never admit it, but I know he is so happy I don't drive.

Well enough of that, this is supposed to be about Dr. Maturi. If we got a cold Mama drowned us in a homemade concoction of Vicks, cough syrup, water and honey. Soon you were better. If you complained you had pains in your legs in the winter you were told it was growing pains. However, for some reason they believed Polio came from the beaches and you would scare them to death. If you had a pain in your side they checked your temperature very carefully, and made sure you weren't throwing up. If all seemed okay, out came the dreaded enema bag. Who needed a doctor when we had one in the house. This was not just our family, but all families. When the doctor was called everyone knew it and it was very serious. You were probably at death's door. We called Dr. Maturi when Jimmy and Mama got sick and one time Mama cut her hand drying a glass. Daddy ran off to the phone at the druggist and along came the doc and fixed everything.

Dr. Maturi's office was on 158th Street which was a block of what they called block houses. When they were first built they were for one family only. Our apartment was the only one on our block. The others were attached block houses. The basement was the kitchen where they had a dumbwaiter to send the food up to the dining room. There was a long flight of stairs up to the front door. Inside on the right were a flight of stairs that went to the bedrooms. However, in later years there were made into apartments. On the left was a large opening and it had pretty wooden scrolling on the top and part of the sides.

I think the first time I went there was when I first got sick with TB. When you went in the left side door you were in the sitting room. It had wooden chairs all along the wall, nothing fancy and no such thing as waiting two weeks for an appointment. You arrived during his office hours, sat down and waited your turn. No one ever tried to steal your turn and everyone, although sick, waited patiently. No complaining to the doctor about how long the wait was. No nurse. He examined you, prescribed whatever, as there really weren't any medications to give except penicillin. The best part comes next, the fee was $3.00 which he put in his pocket. If you gave him a 5 dollar bill he would put it in his pocket and pull out two bills. He would then tell you if you weren't feeling better in a week to ten days to come back to see him. Isn't that great? So simple compared to me working my fingers to the bone typing insurance claim forms and keeping the balances current on the ledgers. He wasn't cheating. It was just the way it was in those days. Later on he moved to a lovely office on the Grand Concourse and actually had a nurse. I am so glad that I was born at a time when I could be a part of these experiences. I will never forget that whole scene and I wasn't surprised at it at all. It was the same everywhere. He got me into a TB hospital and took care of me after and he always came to see my mother to take care of her.

After I married, my mother got an infection in her leg and was admitted to the hospital. The first evening I went to see her I was appalled at the condition of her room and her care. I called Dr. Maturi and asked him if I brought her home would he come to see her and tell me how to take care of her infection. He said of course he would. Peggy and I called an ambulance and she was taken to my house. Huey and I put her in our beautiful bedroom and we slept on the pull out couch. She was so happy.

Dr. Maturi came the next day and I asked if he had any trouble finding the house as we lived in a beautiful big fancy courtyard. He said no, but you didn't tell me you lived on the fifth floor. I asked if he would have come anyway and he said of course he would and complimented me on the way my mother was being taken care of.

THE EYE CLINIC

The first day of school, the teacher knew I needed glasses because I could not see the blackboard. Of course the school nurse gave me an eye exam and informed my mother I definitely needed to get glasses. She gave my mother a slip to the free Eye Clinic. Actually they were very nice, but you always had a long wait and had to sit on wooden benches. They checked me and a week later we went back for the glasses. They were those awful wire rimmed round glasses which were popular for the poor at that time. The doctor was very nice and I remember as I was leaving he told me to be sure to wear them all the time. I said "even when I go to bed?" He laughed and said I could remove them in bed. I was trying to figure out in my mind how I would manage the cot and the glasses.

One time Daddy took Bootsie and me to The Eye Clinic. We had to sit on these high wooden benches and there was a long wait. The other children were running all over the place but, we were sitting like little soldiers until our turn came. No one ever went into a room alone without another family member. Of course Daddy accompanied me and brought Bootsie with him so she would not be alone in the waiting room. Everything went by fine until they asked me to look at this page and tell them what I saw.

No one ever explained to you why you were to do anything. So I didn't know what they wanted. Daddy was watching over my shoulder and I was nervous I might say the wrong thing. He finally encouraged me to answer and I said a 3. They were just checking to see if I was colorblind. He asked me on the way home what took me so long as I certainly knew a 3 when I saw one. I told him I didn't know what to do and didn't want to mess up. He said that he was getting nervous that I might be color blind which is what they were testing me for. It was confusing to be a little child because no one told you anything except for street smarts. You just kind of wandered around and did what you were told.

We didn't have a place to go to if you got an earache. Mama used a piece of cloth and packed it with salt and tied it with string. She then heated it in the frying pan until it was just the right temperature. We held it on our ear until the pain was gone. The same procedure was done for a toothache. You couldn't grow up in the Depression and be a wimp. Kids had pretty thick skins.

THE DENTAL CLINIC

Of course we couldn't afford to go to a real dentist so we went to the dental clinic run by the city. Believe me this was no walk in the park. This was a clinic for children. You walked into a large room with wooden chairs all along the side with one child sitting next to his or her parent. Mama took me this day. Of course you never went unless you were crying with a toothache. Actually you didn't want to go. It was such a dreary place and seemed like a place of torture. If they pulled your tooth they gave you Novocaine. If they just filled a tooth you got zero medication. Actually no dentists did give sedation for a filling. At one end was a wooden wall with glass on top that you could not see through, just as well or you would have run out the door. Inside were five dental chairs all in one room. You were a little child and you were scared to death.

One day Mama and I were sitting waiting for my turn when we heard a roar from the other room. Some little Irish boy yelled out as loud as he could, "You rotten S.O.B., get your filthy hands off me" – only he didn't say S.O.B. The whole room was in shock except for one man whose face was red as a beet, he knew his child. Then the nurse opened the door and announced, "Would Mr. Feeney please come forward and take his son home?" When they left everyone screamed laughing, even the children because they thought it was hilarious and knew how he felt, but would never have the courage to do it.

MAMA'S KITCHEN

Mama's kitchen was the smallest room in the house and everyone hung out there. It was always so cozy and the baking and cooking she did permeated the air. When Peggy and Mary came home from school at night we all brought chairs into the kitchen and had tea and fresh warm home made bread. One time I remember Eddie, Jimmie and I played a game of Monopoly at the table while she was cooking. I don't know how she did it as there certainly weren't any counters like we have today. She used one corner of the table so we had enough room. She seemed to enjoy our company and never chased us into the dining room which had a huge table. She liked us near her and we certainly wanted to be near her.

One day she was making apple pie and I was sitting at the end of the table with my feet on the chair. As she peeled and quartered the apples for the pie she would hand me one. When that was finished she gave me another one.

Somehow we got on the subject of names and she told me her name used to be Gaerth before she got married. I was horrified and highly indignant that she had actually changed her name. It's funny how children can only think so far. Did I think all my friends had their mother's maiden name? She tried to explain to me that that's the way it is because you wanted the whole family to have the same name. That's part of what makes you a family. I said, "Oh no, not me! I am keeping my name. I think Christina Lynch is a beautiful name especially because of how Daddy always speaks of his sister as "my sister Christina." She died young and I was named for her. I will not change that!"

She tried to explain that when I grew up I would meet someone and fall in love. We would get married and I would be happy to share his name. I said, "He can keep his own name and I will keep mine." I pondered what to do because I knew that was never going to happen. Finally I came up with my solution. I said "I know, I'll marry Eddie." She gave up, put her pies in the oven and having solved my problem, I went out to play. Of course Eddie happened to be my brother.

MACOMBS DAM PARK

This park was filled with children all day in the summer. It was right next to the Yankee Stadium and had a track for runners, a basketball court, several baseball fields and a girl's softball team which Doris and I joined and were lucky to get out of alive.

About one block away they had a huge pool which was called "THE KIDDIE POOL." We went there almost every day. Poor Mary, our older sister, had to drag us about 14 blocks in the sweltering heat with us complaining about how hot and thirsty we were.

We did not have plastic water bottles then so you just had to tough it out until you got there and could drink from the water fountain. We brought along towels and wore our bathing suits (I wonder where they came from?) We also brought lunch which was pretty soggy by the time we reached our destination. But, the pool was worth it. It was only ankle deep and got deeper as you waded out to the middle, which was pretty shallow too, but you could swim. We thought we were in heaven. Then we would start the long trek back to 160th Street and then home. Of course we were all sunburned and dripping wet. About one quarter of the way home there was a huge peach tree and we would all grab a big, fat, juicy peach and suck on it, wiping the warm juice running down our chins. What a great time and I am so happy to have the memories.

I TOLD ME DA

Recently I was shopping and I came across an Irish CD. I looked through it to see what songs I didn't already have. I came across one called, "I'll tell me ma." I knew immediately that I would love this because it would be some Irish girl complaining about some boy who was bothering her.

The first two lines were perfect for me as one time I had to go home and tell me Da.

I'll tell me ma when I get home

The byes won't leave the Gerrls alone

(I do know how to spell boys and girls.)

When I was in about sixth grade I had some trouble with the byes. The byes would get to school early and build a snow fort and fill it with snowballs right outside of the entrance and exit we had to use. Then to make it worse they were excused from school five minutes before the Gerrls. Naturally we were bombarded with snow balls and had to run all the way home. If there was one thing I hated it was being hit with snowballs as they really hurt. We got it in the morning and then after school.

One day I went home crying and Me Da asked what was wrong. I told him my tale of woe and he asked me a few questions and I thought that was it. I should have realized Me Da would never let anyone hurt or frighten us.

The next day I came out of school and standing there was Me Da and the byes across the street looked terrified. I haven't any idea what he said to them, but it had to be scary.

I said, "OH DADDY."

I should have known he would be there because if anyone bothered us on the street he would always take care of it. He said "Come on and we will walk home together and no one will throw snowballs at you anymore." He must have gone in to see the principal because after that the Gerrls got dismissed five minutes before the poor old byes.

Strange, but when I was a teenager Huey and his friend Larry used to pummel my friend Doris and me with snowballs the whole winter. One time Huey threw one from a block away and hit me right on the top of my head. I liked the attention but hated the snowballs. Several times we were just walking down the street and suddenly the two of them jumped from behind a car and almost killed us. But I never told Me Da as I didn't want him messing the romance that would develop when Huey finally realized I was the girl he would eventually fall in love with. I knew it would happen someday and I would have to be patient and keep on lighting those candles at St. Peter and Paul's Church. He used to make fun of me for going to church all the time and asked me to say a prayer for him and I would reply, "Oh, I certainly will." Little did he know I was putting my dime in the box and lighting a candle and pray that he would soon like me and ask me out. In another story I will tell how it finally came to pass.

MAMA'S COATS

I used to babysit twins whose father was a tailor. I loved those two little kids. They were so sweet and good and they loved me too. I was also kind of a mother's helper to Mrs. Martin Blank. They also had a boy they called BOOBIE which I assume means little boy. He was two years older than the twins and that's how it all began. I will tell his story a little later.

My mother made a beautiful coat for me and Aunt Nellie Harley's three girls and my sister Bootsie. I think it was the first real coat any of us had. Aunt Nellie had five daughters and very little money, but she somehow managed to get her hands on enough material and trimmings for five coats. It was the best material you could buy and the work my mother put into it was absolutely perfection. She had just enough left over to make a muff for Bootsie and me. Imagine owning a muff then. I felt like we should be on a sleigh ride in Germany someplace. She even put a little pocket in the top with a zipper to close it.

Daddy was so proud that one day he took me to Maldacher's Bar to fill the growler. Mr. Maldacher went crazy over the muff because it reminded him of Germany. He said, "Such a beautiful muff must have a coin in it." He pulled the zipper open and put a nickel in. It was a real sweet moment and I will always remember it.

That Christmas, Mrs. Blank gave me a knitted German hat. It had two large squares attached to it that covered my ears. The squares had roses embroidered on them. There were matching gloves, with the roses on them too.

How about those stockings? They were the new fad. We were so tired of those baby garter belts so someone had the idea to put a rubber band on the top of the stockings and roll them down. We thought we were hot stuff. Even through our thighs and knees were now freezing.

DAS LOUSE BOOB

Martin Blank was only two years old when his mother came home from the hospital with two beautiful babies – a boy and a girl. The whole family was there and made a tremendous fuss over these twins. Martin was called Boobie by everyone and had much attention until these little children were born. He stated with a big pout, "I am going down to see my Papa." Well his papa was a very fine man and a very good father, but he owned a large tailor shop and was very busy making a living for this fine German family. Everyone was German – all their friends and relatives and they were very nice people. The Blanks lived on the second floor of this house over the tailor shop. When you entered the front door you would find yourself in a nice entryway. On each side was a doorway. The right doorway led into the store and the left into the part where he kept all the finished clothes. Straight ahead was a nice wooden staircase leading to their four room apartment. At the top of the stairs were the same doors so you could enter either end and go through the apartment and come out the other end. In later years this became a great escape route for little Boobie.

Something happened that day that wrecked the household. You just never knew what he would do next. His Tanta Rosa loved to knit and I remember one time when she left the room and put down a sweater she had almost finished knitting. Boobie took a pair of scissors and cut it all the way up the back, right next to the knitting needles. Sometimes when someone got up to walk across the room he would tackle them. One time his father went out to get the milk and papers from outside the front door. Boobie locked the door behind him. It was wintertime and Mr. Blank was in his pajama pants and a tee shirt. Boobie was in the tailor shop window making all kinds of faces at him. He used to sneak down to the room where the clothes were ready to pick up and change all the tickets. People didn't have phones at that time, Mr. Blank would just write their names on a piece of paper and pin it to the item. They were all in alphabetical order, but Boobie would change all the tickets. So, if you dropped off an overcoat, Mr. Blank might find a pair of pants with our name on it. All of a sudden we would hear a roar, "DAS LOUSE BOOB, Boobie would come flying up the stairs in those little chubby German legs with his father flying after him. I would grab the twins and take them out of the line of fire while the other two flew around the house in and out of each door. On the fourth trip Boobie would make a slide just like an expert baseball player under his parents' bed. When he got into the middle Mr. Blank couldn't reach him. I always wondered why Mr. Blank didn't think to stop halfway and catch him as he turned a corner. But, he was in such a rage he couldn't even think straight. He then had to go through all the clothes until the customer had his proper merchandise. Mr. Blank did most of the tailoring and I remember him sitting in the window of the shop on his treadle sewing machine for hours. He was such a hard worker. He had a man who pressed all the clothes which were kept in a big bin and Boobie would hide in the bin and then jump out and scare the poor man half to death.

One Easter morning I ran around the corner to give all three children chocolate Easter bunnies. Everything was going fine until I heard a woman scream. I ran into the living room just in time to see Boobie getting down from the windowsill after peeing on a neighbor's brand new Easter Bonnet as she was walking to church. I got out of there as fast as I could.

Well Boobie grew up to be one of the nicest boys you could hope to know. He loved his mother with all his heart and couldn't do enough for her. She had sent him to a German Catholic School, and they straightened him out in about two weeks.

Later, they moved to 156th Street. They didn't need a babysitter any more but I would still go and visit her quite often. She was one of the nicest people I ever knew. I remember she also used to say, "Why did I have to have such kids" I used to laugh because the twins were wonderful.

When the twins were babies my sister Mary used to take care of them. Then when she was busy in school and working I was fortunate to take over. Boobie never did anything to me, because I took him with me wherever I took the twins. I remember we would play in the snow and then come in and sit by her big coal stove to warm our feet and Mrs. Blank would make us hot chocolate. The house was always full of first generation German speaking people. I actually got to know and speak German quite well.

One of my fondest memories was when Mrs. Blank would do her laundry. She had a nice machine that she filled with water and it did the washing for her. Then she ran the clothes through the ringer to rinse them. How I wished Mama had a machine like that. She was still doing wash for nine people on a washboard bent over a deep laundry sink. I would then climb out her kitchen window and stand on the roof next door and hand the wet laundry on a line that ran from her kitchen window, to the house next door. This roof looked down on our kitchen and living room windows. I would call to Mama and she would come to the window and wave to me and then Daddy would come to the living room window and wave and say, "Be careful now don't get too close to the edge." I can still feel the cold sheets wrapping around me and hitting me in the face. They smelled so clean and fresh. I spent a lot of time with Mrs. Blank and she was so nice to me. I helped her with the cleaning, all the German cooking, her ironing and just visiting with her was such a pleasure.

THE ICE MAN

In the 1930's we kept our food fresh in an ice box. To keep the ice box cold we would buy a big block of ice from the local "Ice Man." He was an Italian and worked very hard. When I think now of his carrying chunks of ice to all the families in our neighborhood, I realize how hard his job really was. In our building we had twenty apartments, four on each floor, and he had to make those trips for each family. He could only carry one piece of ice at a time because they were so heavy.

He would pull his truck to the curb. Then he pulled himself onto the bed of the truck and peeled back a large, thick canvas to expose a huge square of ice. Using a long, sharp ice pick, he chipped a straight line of holes where he wanted to separate the ice from the larger block. By this time the neighborhood kids would be all around waiting for him to get finished. He would chase us away a bit because he didn't want anyone to get chips of ice on them. He gripped the ice with large metal tongs. He placed a large piece of rubber over his shoulder and then hoisted the ice onto his shoulder and carried it into each apartment. As soon as he was gone we all scrambled to get the pieces that had broken and had a delicious cold treat which was very welcome on the hot steaming streets of the Bronx. Can you imagine a child today being thrilled to consider it a treat to suck on a ragged piece of ice? They would think you were completely out of your mind.

Our wooden icebox, lined with metal, contained a compartment at the top for the ice, which was admitted through a separate hinged door. The lower door opened to expose shelves for holding food.

As the ice melted, the water drained through a hose into a pan under the icebox. This water was very cold and had to be emptied often. My parents were particularly vigilant about this because my mother's little sister once played in the water and got pneumonia and died.

In the winter we had a metal cabinet outside our kitchen window. I haven't any idea how it was attached but it had two sliding doors so we could reach in to extract the perishables. That way we saved the money on the ice.

Our landlord installed refrigerators in each apartment so that ended the career of the iceman. He was a very hard worker and very kind to the children who bugged him for ice and we really liked him. When he came around everyone would come running and screeching with delight, "HERE COMES THE ICE MAN."

Life was simple back then. It took very little to please a child. I still remember the sweet, simple memories and those who made them possible.

OFF TO WAR

I remember when Buddy went into the Navy during the war. We were all so sad, but I think it was the hardest on my sister Peggy. They were so close and I can still remember how hard she cried that morning. He was the first to leave home and it was very hard to see a member of the family go off to war. He was in school for a while, but then went off to the Pacific. He went out in the destroyers that left first to look for Japanese submarines. We put a star in the window to honor him. It was a blue star on a piece of cloth. The top had a string on it and this was hung onto a little clasp that locked the top and bottom windows. Almost every apartment had one hanging in the window and many had three, four and five stars on the same piece of cloth. If a serviceman died, the blue star was replaced with a gold star. It was very sad to see a gold star. I have the two stars my Aunt Mary put in her window for her husband and my father during World War I.

I remember my mother would wait for Buddy's letters. The one who went to the mailbox would come running into the apartment yelling, "We got a letter." When he went overseas you could see the colorful airmail envelope through the slots in the mailbox and you were so happy to know he was all right. My parents would read the letter to the ones at home and it would then be put up on the refrigerator for those who came home later.

I remember when he would get leave. I would sit on the front steps and wait for him to come down the street. Soon, I would see the tall sailor coming down the street and I would run and throw my arms around him. How tall and handsome he was in his sailor's uniform. Hunter High School had a "Serviceman's Beauty Contest." Peggy and Mary entered Buddy's picture and he won "Most Handsome Serviceman." We were all so proud.

For a while he got leave every weekend. He brought two sailor friends with him. They slept at the YMCA and spent a lot of time at our house. On Sunday afternoon my parents would send me to the bakery for three dozen butter cookies. They were little round or oblong cookies with dabs of chocolate on them. They were expensive and delicious. The bakery lady would put them in a box tied with string and I would carry them home taking great care not to break any.

THE AIR RAID DRILLS

During World War II we always had air raid tests but we never knew when they would be. They were just tests to help us prepare in case someday we really would get bombed. It was kind of scary for us kids. If the air raid siren sounded during the daytime when we were at school, everyone had to get under their desks, but if it happened at nighttime you had to put out all of the lights throughout the whole city. You could not have a candle or even the slightest light, because if the Germans or the Japanese were looking for a target, they could see any kind of a light.

One night I was roller skating with my friend Kathryn Korinus and the air raid siren started. She went in her house and asked if I wanted to come in. I said, "No, my father will be looking for me and if he can't find me he is going to be frantic and if I go in and close the door, he won't know where to find me." So all the lights went out and I just stayed by her house in the pitch dark, but I knew he would come and get me; he was so protective of us. He had a terrible temper, but he was so loving. You could go to him with any kind of problem and he would help you solve it.

I was by her house, just standing there on my roller skates and I heard, "Dena, Dena, where are you?" I said, "I'm at Kathryn Korinus's house." I knew he would come. I stayed there and he said, "Don't move, stay right where you are, I am coming to get you right now." I just stayed there. Then he came and told me to take my skates off and we just waited until the air raid siren stopped because it was pitch dark. I don't know how he even found me. He wouldn't have if I was in somebody's house and he would have been frantic. So he walked me home, and as soon as he was with me, I felt so calm. He told me I did a good job by staying in one place and trusting that he would come.

That is a nice story I think. Whenever there was a problem he was there for you. The second sirens would go off and the air raid warden would come out, he would turn the lights back on, and it was always nice to have the lights on again.

ROSIE THE RIVETER

During the war Mama got a job in a defense plant. She made spark plugs for airplanes. If I can remember correctly, she worked nights down in Manhattan. She was home when we were leaving for school. She loved the job and her independence. We called her Rosie the Riveter. She wanted to help the war effort and bring some money home. It was quite a step for her to take a job. When the war ended every street was blocked, and someone provided music and all the neighbors danced in the street. Every house had a roman candle on the front steps.

Another time she showed her independence was during voting time. Women in those days mostly voted as their husband's did. But, Peggy was going to college and coming home with some "radical ideas." She started telling Mama that women should vote the way they wanted, not just how their husband voted. The story goes that Mama voted for the other candidate. I thought she was probably the bravest woman in the world.

I doubt that Daddy ever found out or perhaps she just voted his way anyway. She loved him very much and would never do anything to deceive him. One time Daddy asked Buddy how he voted and Buddy said that it was suppose to be a secret ballot. That ended that!!!

THE ITALIAN DINNER

I loved people and was drawn to them. I was friends with whole families in our neighborhood. I would call for a friend and if she wasn't home, her mother would invite me in for a cup of tea. I liked all the different nationalities and their diverse customs. Once at Peggy's house we were talking about the old days, and she asked, "Who are all these people you are talking about? I never heard of them." I told her I was very friendly with them all. She worked in the day to support us and went to school at night. I was out talking to people on the street all the time.

My Italian friend, Mary, invited me to Sunday Dinner at her house. Of course I knew here two sisters and her father very well and was very pleased to see what favorite meals they prepared. Wow, was I in for a surprise.

We started out with antipasto, which is all kinds of delicatessen meats. I was surprised because I thought they would have more Italian food. When they cleared the table they brought out a huge plate of spaghetti and meatballs. I ate as much as I could, as I wanted to be polite, but I was stuffed. Then they cleared the table and out came the turkey. My eyes almost popped out of my head. How could I possibly eat all of this? All the while we were eating they were filling my water glass with what was called Guinea Red which is what everyone called Italian homemade wine. The father was so proud of his wine that he kept filling up my glass. I was about twelve years old. I don't know where he got the grapes or how he made it, but it was stored somewhere in that apartment because he kept bringing out big jugs of it. I have no idea what they had for dessert, but I doubt I could eat it. I don't know where they got the money from for such a feast as this is the way they ate every Sunday. They probably had some friends offering them something they couldn't refuse. After dinner I had to walk three blocks home a wee bit dizzy.

THE NEW TELEVISION

We were the first family in the neighborhood to have a TV set. Buddy made us a little TV, it didn't even have a cabinet around it. We put it in the bedroom and only Buddy and Mama could operate it. Buddy was afraid that someone might get electrocuted on all the open wires. The only one he trusted was Mama. Word soon got around that we had one of those new TV sets. The neighbors would come in on Tuesday evenings to see "Milton Berle – Mr. Television." Sitting on the bed and in chairs around the room you would see Mrs. Donnelon and her mother from 1A. Mrs. Bissonette, her daughter and mother from 1D, and Mrs. Waters and her sister Josephine from 4C. They would have beer and pretzels and have a great time. The bedroom was filled with people in awe of this new invention and to think that Buddy made it!

JAMES FRANCIS LYNCH

Jimmie was our brother. He was fifteen months older than I was and we were great friends. I missed him terribly when he went to school. He was such a sweet little boy and such a hard worker. He and our brother Eddie were very young when they worked after school. They worked at a grocery store and I remember that they did not have a cash register. They had to add up all the purchases that were made on a paper bag the groceries were put in. I was amazed at how he could add so many numbers. I think the store was Gristedes. It was on Elton Avenue. One day they decided that they would open a larger store called SAFEWAY. They could not have two people from the same family working in the store. Jimmie applied to Grand Union and was hired immediately. He worked there for a long time. My brothers always watched out for me. We used to play a game called "KNUCKS." It was a card game and the loser had to make a fist, while all the other players hit the loser on the knuckles. My brothers would barely hit me and when it came time for the others they would remind them whom they were hitting. They were pretty tough Irish kids so they were pretty much left alone.

Jimmie saved his money and purchased a two-wheeler bike. Before he got the bike we used to go to a store that rented bikes by the hour. I didn't learn to ride one until I was sixteen years old. Jimmie knew I loved it and let me use the bike anytime I wanted. My whole family was so good to each other. I remember the boys showing me how to flip baseball cards and play marbles.

I was surprised when I looked through my box of pictures that I had so many pictures of Jimmie. Then it came back to me. Raymond Bissonette lived next door to us and his mother was the janitor. There were several empty bins in the basement and she allowed them to use one as a dark room. They bought a camera and developed their own pictures. They had learned how in school. They would let me take and develop pictures. It was lots of fun watching the pictures slowly develop and hanging them on a string hung across the room. We used old-fashioned clothespins to hold them in place.

Jimmie was also sentimental, as the Irish tend to be. Mary was the first to get married and I remember one night about two months later he said, "It's just not the same without Mary. I really miss her."

We lost our three brothers and Mary in just seven years. It was so heartbreaking. I am so glad we stayed close through all the years.

When Jimmie was just a young boy, he came down with meningitis. He was sick and we called the doctor who thought he just had the grippe, which is what we called the flu back then. There really wasn't much they could do. Jimmie just kept getting worse and was complaining about the pain in his neck and eyes. Daddy ran two blocks to the police station to call for an ambulance. It must have been at the beginning of the war as we had Air Raids where all the lights in the city were turned off and poor Jimmie woke up in one and though he had gone blind. He was screaming and the nurse assured him it would be over very soon. You could not wander in and out of the hospital like you can today. They had strict visiting hours, but my father sneaked up the outside metal stairs every night and brought him some treats or ice cream. He just couldn't stand to have Jimmie there all alone and nothing was going to keep him out. I guess the stairs were in case they should have to evacuate people on stretchers.

Eddie had a problem one time where he was throwing up blood, so my parents took him to the same hospital. He used to drink milk straight from the bottle at work and they think he must have swallowed a piece of glass, So Daddy made the same trip up the stairs at night. All our friends went to see him and one girl gave him the book, "Forever Amber." It was considered the most salacious book at the time and my mother had a fit. She could not understand how a girl could possibly do such a terrible thing. She actually thought it would make his blood pressure rise. All the teenagers were reading it. Believe me, by today's standards it was very mild. It was so popular that they made a motion picture of it. Poor Mama was horrified that someone would give him such a book, as a matter of fact, I don't even know how she knew about it.

JIMMIE THE HERO

For a while Jimmie worked the night shift with another fellow at Grand Union. I don't know what their jobs were, but they had to go into the freezer. Jimmie went in and the other fellow followed him and let the door shut behind him. Jimmie was very careful to not let this happen because the door, when closed, could only be opened from the outside. They couldn't get out and they would be in there all night and freeze to death.

But Jimmie was very strong and was determined to open the door. The other fellow sat in the corner saying prayers. Jimmie told him that somehow they were getting out of there. They wouldn't have been found until the morning. Jimmie stood at the back of the freezer wall and ran with all his energy and kicked the door. The lock was huge and strong. It took him more than an hour, but he finally broke the lock and they were freed. He then insisted they install a lock that you could open from the inside. When he came home the next day and told us what had happened, we were all upset to think he was in such danger and we weren't even aware of it.

CHRISTINA LYNCH MEETS EUGENE HILGENBERG

I met Huey when I first entered high school. It was April and I was three months into my freshman year. I was only fourteen and he was fifteen. His best friend, Larry, brought him into the neighborhood. He really lived only three blocks away but I had never seen him before. Doris and I were walking to the store when I saw Larry and stopped to say hello. There were quite a few boys and girls in a circle joking around. I knew them all except for Huey. He was at the other end of the circle with his back to me when he suddenly turned around and I almost couldn't breathe because I knew that he was the one I was going to marry. There have been many times in my life when I just knew things. I think it is an Irish trait because my grandmother did too. They are very superstitious and think it has something to do with "The Little People" and they call anyone who has a sixth sense FAY.

Of course we were all so sophisticated that Larry didn't even introduce us. Doris and I went on our way and I told her I was going to marry the blonde boy. I wondered what his name was. I was not boy crazy and did not really want to be bothered with them except for this one.

A group of us went to Coney Island one day and the boys and girls started to pair off. Well Huey was not the least bit interested in me. Larry paired off with Dorothy who was best friends with Margaret. I never could understand what he saw in her as she had fat hips and Bugs Bunny teeth. Well I might be exaggerating a bit, but her teeth were definitely bucked. She had braces which she threw down the incinerator. I guess they interfered with all the kissing she did. She dated most every boy in the neighborhood including both my brothers and Huey. They didn't really go on dates – just sort of hung around together – but they were definitely going together. Around one year later Huey decided he didn't want to see her any more as he just wanted to play baseball. I was very happy, but it didn't help me in any way. Actually it was good because if you date someone in high school chances are you will not marry that person. I had to wait four years for him to notice me. In the meantime I would not date anyone because someday he was going to be mine.

We went to all the dances we could find as I loved to dance. If a boy asked me out I told him my parents wouldn't let me date until I was eighteen. As I looked through these stories I am a little surprised to realize lies rolled out of my mouth pretty easily.

THE ALPINE GIRLS

Many years ago when Doris and I were teenagers we played softball. It was under the auspices of the Police Athletic League (PAL) organized to keep the boys and girls actively involved in sports and out of trouble. A man named John Brum was in charge of the P.A.L. in our area.

The boys were called "The Elton Eagles" and the girls were "The Alpine Girls." I never liked that name as it had nothing to do with the Bronx. The boys were from Elton Avenue, so their name fit, but ours didn't. Brum was in charge of the boys and his wife was in charge of the girls. We always called him Brum, but his wife was always Mrs. Brum. I guess the guys wanted to act tough around him.

One summer day Doris and I didn't have much to do so we walked over to Macoomb's Dam Park because that's where all the action was. We sat on the benches to watch the girls play a softball game. Soon Huey and his best friend Larry came along and sat behind us. We both really liked them, but they were only interested in baseball. Suddenly behind us we started to hear "Wow, look at her arm, that one can really hit, look a home run, wow – a great double play! These girls are great!" etc. So, we looked at each other and made a plan. We thought if we played ball they would show some interest in us.

We walked over to Brum and asked if we could try out for the team and he agreed to talk it over with his wife. She agreed and we were thrilled, but not for very long. I thought they would put us out in the outfield and we could grab a ball now and then. The started us in the infield- I was about five foot three inches and weighed 115 lbs. and Doris was five feet and weighted 100 lbs. Everyone else was about five seven and weight about 165 lbs, and all of it muscle! Doris was shortstop and I was first baseman. To make matters worse the girls hated us because they wanted to win the Championship game and knew darn well they didn't have a chance with these two babies out there. I stood on first base and prayed no one would throw or hit anything near me. Where was my brain--everything goes to first base and Doris got hit in the face with the ball and almost lost her front teeth. Besides that we had to go to all kinds of practices. These girls threw the ball as hard as they could. I was afraid I would get a broken hand. I could hit pretty well, but was always trying to stay out of the way of the ball. The pitcher was a monster. I finally realized they gave us these positions so we would get the heck out of there. We played four games, always in danger of injury. I told Doris every day that I wanted out. My parents didn't have money for surgery.

She loved it and didn't want to leave. I wanted to support her, but I knew we were in trouble. The end came the day we arrived for practice and we were going to be taught to slide into the bases. I could just picture that size 10 foot right in my face. That was the day Doris almost got hurt sliding into second. I told her I would come to all her games and cheer for her, but I was glad to be out of there. She left too.

I found out later that the last girls either Larry or Huey ever would have been interested in were **BIG MUSCULAR GIRLS**. I guess lighting all those candles at church saved us as they never saw one of our games.

THE LOT

We had a big empty lot at the end of my street where many of the kids played softball and other games. The boys used to roast Mickies, which were raw potatoes. They would build a good fire and throw the potatoes in until they were cooked. I thought they tasted awful, but some of the kids were probably pretty hungry and liked them and the adventure of the fire. We would never go near the fire as Daddy could smell it as soon as you were in the door and he was very frightened of fire.

Doris, some friends of ours and I decided we would start playing baseball in the lot. I wasn't about to face The Alpine Girls again. One day Doris pitched a beautiful ball to me and I swung hard at it and it flew right through a second story window over Maldacher's Beer Garden. Everyone's first reaction was to run as fast as possible. I dropped my bat and flew around the corner to my own house. Of course I knew I would have to go in and tell Daddy what happened as he knew everyone in the bar and everyone knew me. Actually, he would not get mad at us if we told the truth, but if we told a lie we were in deep trouble, especially if someone in the street told on us.

So I went in the apartment and explained what happened. He said "A second floor window eh?" and he told me not to worry about it. He would go up to the Beer Garden, buy the man a drink and pay for the window. As he was leaving I said, "Daddy do you think you could get my ball-- it's in someone's kitchen?" He asked me if there was anything else I would like and I had the nerve to tell him my bat was still in the lot. He told me to get my own bat and he would take care of the ball. He kind of shook his head when he went out the door. But I had to ask; after all it was our only ball! Later he asked me to please go over to Macoomb's Dam Park where all the baseball fields were and there were no windows around and I would be safe.

After that we started riding bicycles. There was a store on Melrose Avenue where you could rent a bike for about ten cents and keep it for hours. We rode those bikes all over the Bronx, weaving in and out of trolley cars and trucks. That was really dangerous, but we flew everywhere and could feel the wind blowing in our faces and through our long curls. Jimmie saved up and bought a bike and let me use it almost all the time. He was so generous because he knew how much I enjoyed it ,another good and loving brother. We Lynches were very blessed.

CASCADE POOL

The elevated train that was east of Yankee Stadium ran up Jerome Avenue. When we rode on it we could see right into CASCADE POOL. It was absolutely big and beautiful and we could look right into it. We were teenagers then and had out grown the kiddy pool and there weren't any other pools we could go to. Of course, this was not a free ride. It cost about fifty cents to get in and who had that much money? We promised ourselves that someday we would mange to get into that pool. Finally, we saved all our money and got tickets into the pool. Oh it was like Heaven! We spent all day jumping off the side and swimming around in the water. Doris was swimming; I was the big baby splashing around because I was terrified of the deep water. Well, this one day I decided I was going to be brave and learn to swim. I went down the ladder in the nine foot end, held on to the side and pushed myself off. I actually did swim a little bit, but suddenly I panicked and realized I could not touch the bottom. How did I ever think I was going to touch bottom in that water? Doris pulled me over to the side and I was done with swimming. I think I would have been better off having someone take me down to the docks and throw me in the East River. I wouldn't be a baby then. That would toughen anyone up.

ENTERTAINMENT

When my parents would go to a movie they would stop in at Maldacher's back room to enjoy a little refreshment. A few times I saw Buddy in there with his friends and Peggy. I would stop in with my best friend, Doris, pull up a chair and they would buy us a Coke with a cherry in it. Doris had a mad crush on my brother Buddy.

Going to the movies could get pretty exciting. The ticket taker would save your ticket stub and at the end of the show they would have a raffle. I can't remember how often this happened, perhaps once a month. One night Mama won a huge box of Pond's Beauty Products. It was in a beautiful satin case and we thought it was gorgeous. As my mother was returning to her seat she saw Daddy going to the stage to receive a 10 dollar prize! One night Eddie and Mary came home with two huge bags filled with groceries. That was cause for excitement in the heart of the Depression.

There was a movie theater on The Grand Concourse near Fordham Road that I believe was called "The Paradise." It was huge, beautiful and very expensive. If a boy took you to this theater you knew he was serious!

You could also collect dishes when you went to the movie theater. Wednesday night was dish night. If you had a friend or cousin getting married and she needed dishes several people would go to the show with her and pick up six dishes. Next week they would get soup bowls etc., until she had a full set of dishes.

THE BUNGALOW

The summer I was about sixteen we rented a bungalow on Staten Island. My father's sister, my Aunt Mary, had rented one too, but she and her only grandson Billy spent all of their time at our Bungalow, and only used theirs for sleeping. Billy's mother, Gicki, would come down on the weekends to spend time with all of us.

We had a great time that summer. Mary met a boy named Ziggy Olejarski who had won a new yellow convertible. We made him take us all for rides. Mary was not interested In Ziggy, she just liked being seen in the new yellow convertible.

Everyone would come down for the weekends. We brought all our friends. All the boys slept on the porch, the girls in the one large bedroom and our parents in the other bedroom. Mama made curtains and bedspreads and fixed it up so it was very clean and pleasant. We had beach parties on Saturday nights. My parents and Aunt Mary cooked the whole weekend and they loved it. Eddie had a friend we called "Hermie the Germie", who ate everything in sight. One Sunday after a very large breakfast, my father jokingly asked Herman if he would like some more to eat. Herman said it would be nice to have six more eggs with some of the delicious bacon and a few more pieces of toast. We almost all fell off our chairs and Aunt Mary who was standing behind Herman was making faces.

There was a cartoon called "Pete the Tramp" in our local paper. Pete was always staling pies from the windowsills where they were put to cool. One day Mama made four lemon pies. She always made a small one for Billie, Aunt Mary's grandson, because it was his favorite pie. Buddy sneaked in the house and unhooked the screen while Jimmie and Eddie stole the pies. Mama was shocked when she went to get her pies and they were all gone. We all had a good laugh while the boys went to get the pies from their hiding place.

Jimmie and Buddy had an old car with a rumble seat in the back. We would head down to Staten Island Ferry with my friend, Doris and me in the rumble seat singing our hearts out. We would drive onto the ferry and stand on the railing of the ferry with the boys. The ferry ride was exhilarating and of course to see the Statue of Liberty up so close!

The following year Buddy found us a bungalow on Lake Hopatcong in New Jersey. I think it was Garrity who was behind this move. That was when Buddy met his future wife Joan. She was a waitress in one of the restaurants across the lake. One night Garrity took us across to the restaurant in his speed boat. That was the first time we met Joan and we could see that Buddy was smitten. He spent a lot of time that summer on the opposite end of the lake. We were warned to behave ourselves as this was very important to him. My mother loved Joan instantly.

My parents again spent the weekend cooking as we had all our friends visiting. One weekend we had an office party. Peggy and Mary worked at Home Life and invited the whole office.

Carol Ann Waters, a neighbor of ours, loved being with us and spent her whole summer in both bungalows because her mother was working.

MUSIC

Buddy loved playing music and when he came home after the war he bought a piano. I think he had a job at the Motorola Music Store and that was where he got the piano. He could play and so could Mama. Unfortunately, our next door neighbor, Mr. Bissonette, also loved the piano.

On summer evenings with the windows open he could hear the strains of the piano. One evening, after a couple of glasses of wine, he had the courage to knock on our door and ask if he could play a few notes. The first time he came we didn't know he had played for silent movies. He would start a nice tune and then suddenly change into something dramatic and then go on to something else. He didn't know any song all the way through. We thought it was hilarious. Once he got in he would stay for hours. Soon you would hear Daddy say to Mama, "Get him out of here. I want to listen to the 10 o'clock news." It got a little scary after that because you never knew if Daddy might throw him out. He never did, but I think he came close a few times.

When we got our first victrola the "jam" sessions began. There was this place on Third Avenue called the "Home for Homeless Boys." They sold used furniture and the proceeds were for the boys' care. A lot of people lost their furniture during the Depression and they had beautiful pieces of furniture. I wanted to buy it all. But we went there for a wind-up victrola and found a gorgeous mahogany one. We then went to the Motorola Music Company and bought some records. We bought a Dorsey Brother's, a Bing Crosby and a recording of Strauss Waltzes. We played them over and over again until we could afford to buy more. We would invite friends and they would bring their records. We would push all the furniture out of the living/dining room and dance away.

When the victrola was delivered in the Home for Homeless Boys truck, Jimmy and Eddie ran and hid for several hours. They thought the home had come for them as they were often warned that they would be headed there if they didn't behave.

Eventually the victrola was replaced with an electric model that you could actually pile several records on at once.

Buddy then started a band. There were French doors separating the living room and the big bedroom. We would open these and the band would set up in the front of the bedroom. Buddy played the guitar, a little skinny guy called "Peanuts" played the drums, Harold Shenke played the trumpet, and Bill Brennen played the base fiddle. Garry Saunders played too, but I can't remember which instrument. Sometimes Garry would bring his girlfriend who later became his wife. Her name was Lee and we all thought she was gorgeous. Buddy had a good friend who lived on our street. Her name was Betty Schmitmeyer and she was a real "BABE." She really liked Buddy, but he liked her only as a friend. She went on to RN school at Bellevue and married a doctor.

Buddy's friend, Victor, didn't play any instrument, but he really loved to dance and was a great dancer. He and I were really great together and used to dance "til all hours" Once he talked about entering the Harvest Moon Ball, but I was too young. I am sure now that he was saying that to make me feel special. Anyway, Victor, liked Peggy, but Peggy was only interested in going to school, that's what made her the happiest. The thing that was so much fun was that we all liked each others' friends. Age didn't matter, and we boogied and waltzed away many an evening.

At this time someone left a xylophone and put it in the bedroom where he had his band, which was right outside my father's door. Everyone who went passed it had to play it. One day Daddy yelled, "Can't anyone in this house go passed that damned thing without banging on it!!!" That was the end of the xylophone.

MRS. WINTER

Victor, as did many of our friends, spent almost all of his time at our house. He was an only child and loved all the activity going on with us. His mother was a nurse who took care of new babies coming home from the hospital. She was very strict, stern and authoritative. As young as I was I knew I wouldn't want her taking care of any of our babies.

One day Mrs. Winter knocked on our door. My mother invited her in and she said she just had to meet us as Victor constantly talked about all the Lynches and loved Mrs. Lynch. She just had to see for herself what Victor found so inviting at our house that he wanted to be there all the time.

I guess Mrs. Winter was happy there too as she soon started dropping in occasionally at lunch time. Mama would send me to the German Deli to get Knockwurst, pickles, potato salad and cake. She would make a big pot of tea and we would sit around the kitchen table having lunch. As soon as Daddy heard Mrs. Winter's voice he grabbed his newspaper and headed for the bedroom. He didn't like bossy Mrs. Winter any better than sentimental Mr. Bissonette.

I would watch my angel mother in her little cotton house dress and Mrs. Winter in her tweed suit and silk blouse. Mrs. Winter would tell Mama how she trained all the babies at six months by holding them over the toilet. My mother would just smile. I would think of Mama gently brushing the boys' hair before they went to school. She did this every day until they were just too tall. Before they came to this country Victor was in the Hitler Youth. I was very happy to have Mama.

115

25TH WEDDING ANNIVERSARY

The year my parents were married 25 years we all chipped in and bought my mother a silver bracelet. Each link was engraved with flowers and our names. There were seven links starting with Peggy down to Bootsie. We gave my father an album (a recording) of all the important events from 1900 to 1940. It contained the live voices on the radio of Lou Gehrig's farewell speech at Yankee Stadium, the announcements of the wars, the Hindenburg explosion, etc. Poor Daddy cried through the whole thing. We didn't know what to do. We just didn't understand why it affected him that way. But now I understand very well. Just typing this makes me cry. When we look at the history of our lives, we can't help but feel the swelling emotions of past experiences, sweet and sad, and departed loved ones so very missed and suddenly we realize we have grown old, a situation that youth thinks will never come.

MY FIRST DATE

I had a friend I grew up with from when I was four years old. I was now sixteen and had avoided any dates. But Donald was a good friend and he was crazy about me, so I usually stayed clear of him. But, this one day he caught me off guard and asked me to the movie. I didn't have the heart to say no, but was sorry the minute I agreed. I didn't want to encourage him in any way. My mother liked him because he liked me so much and he was Catholic.

Saturday night arrived and I was dying. He called for me and I wasn't quite ready, but there was a mirror I was looking in that reflected what was going on in the living room. He was the most polite person in the world, but way over the top. From the reflection in the mirror I could see Peggy get up to get a pair of scissors from the table, they were always sewing) and Don jumped up to be polite. I could see Peggy give Mary a funny look and I thought "Oh No! Don't do it!" When Peggy sat, he sat. Then Mary stood up and he jumped up again. Peggy and Mary kept that up for about 5 minutes and from where I was getting ready it looked like popcorn popping all over the living room! When my mother walked into the room he jumped so high I thought he would hit his head on the ceiling! I got out of there as fast as I could. Mary and Peggy told me later that they had to make some fun out of it, as they were jealous because I had a date and they were sitting home sewing!

We then left the house and headed to 161st St. for the bus and around the corner were Huey and Larry making fun of us. "Going on a date huh? You must be going to the movie. What are you going to see?" Buses come about every five minutes in the Bronx, but not ours. No bus for forty five minutes! They started again: "Why don't you take a cab? Maybe you don't have enough money. I could lend you some." I wanted to walk, but he said the movie would start before we could get there. Finally we were rescued. I was never so happy to get on a bus. I sat with arms folded through the whole movie so he couldn't hold my hand. On the way home he insisted we stop for a hot chocolate. They we had one block to get back to my house. I thought, what am I going to do? Will he just walk me to the steps and say goodnight or will he want to walk me to the apartment door? Suppose he tries to kiss me? I will just have to escape and get right in the house. " We turned the corner and there sitting on the stoop was Daddy. He never sat on the stoop, but he knew his nutty daughter needed help. Donald said, "Good evening Mr. Lynch" and to me: "I really had a nice time." I said, "Thank you Daddy." And we went in the house. I realized he knew I was a wreck because I didn't want to go out and wouldn't know how to handle myself on a first date.

FAT CHARLIE

Huey pitched or played short stop and Fat Charlie was the catcher. Well, I promised myself I would never be caught off guard if someone asked me out. One day Fat Charlie told me he had box seat tickets to that afternoon's Yankee game. I never sat in box seats. They were only three rows back and near the Yankee Dugout. The game was with the Boston Red Socks. There was no way I could go alone with him as the whole neighborhood would say I was Fat Charlie's girlfriend, but I was ready this time. I asked him how many tickets he had and said he had three. BINGO. I immediately replied that it was wonderful because Doris could go too. I couldn't possibly go without her as she loved the Yankees as much as I did. He didn't seem too pleased, but what could he say. We went and had a wonderful time. I did feel a little sorry for him but if I went alone with him I would be tortured forever. How could I want everyone to tease me that bad?

Honestly, my choice was to go on a date with Fat Charlie or be willing to wait for the knuckle head Huey to wake up and realize I was a girl. I decided to wait. I knew it would happen someday for hadn't the angels told me so?

REMEMBERING OUR OLD NEIGHBORHOOD

Dena dearest companion
Of childhood days,
We traded baseball cards, rode homemade scooters
And put on plays.

The New York streets

Teemed with children in those long ago times,

And were the best places for games,

Like statues and mimes.

The sidewalks vibrated

With the happiest noise,

Yells, screams, and laughter,

From girls and boys.

Our block was the center

In every way

It was where everyone gathered,

To run and play.

It's hard to describe,

The love we all felt,

For our old Bronx neighbors,

And Franklin Roosevelt.

We loved God, country,

And the American flag,

And we played a lot of stoop-ball,

Stick ball, kick the can and tag.

We also loved pizza, the Yankees,

And the Good Humor Man;

Orchard Beach was a must,

We all wanted a tan,

On, days of jump rope,

Roller skates, and jacks,

To the years spent at Melrose,

'Neath the orange and the black (school colors)

Most of us went to,

Old Public School Number Three,

A relic left over,

From the last century.

We pledged to each other,

On graduation day,

That no matter how far apart,

Our paths may stray.

We would never forget

Public School #3 (orange and black)

As forward we marched,

Into eternity.

Blessed be the days,

Gone by,

St. Peter and Paul,

To you we cry.

Church of our childhood,

The Catholic dream,

Of purity, perfection,

And souls so clean.

Oh Dena, do you remember,

The songs we used to sing?

From East One Hundred and Sixtieth Street,

Our voices would ring.

We sang East Side, West Side,

The song of Mamie O'Rourke

As we tripped the light fantastic,

On the sidewalks of New York.

Dena if this poem should ever reach you,

Somehow, someway,

There's one last thing left to say:

Thank God, for you, New York, and yesterday.

Yours Always,

Doris Hendrick Rojas – My very best friend, even today.

THE HEIST

It was a nice warm summer day and Doris and I were sitting on the curb wondering if we could think of how we could earn some money to go to Cascade Pool. When, like magic the Italian Green Grocer right across from my apartment house came out and asked if we could run an errand for him, as he was alone in the store and couldn't leave. He said someone from the house on 159th Street needed some groceries and change of a $20.00 bill. We said we knew the house and he said he would give us a tip. He told us the people lived on the sixth floor. We went in and pushed the button for #6 and it stopped at #4. The door opened and we were greeted by three Puerto Rican boys. Because my father taught us every street smart known to mankind, I knew we were in trouble and this was a setup. I pushed Doris right out of the elevator, as we weren't going to stay in that enclosed place with these hoods. Doris was a real ditz and didn't get any of what was happening. She was asking me what I was doing while one of the boys pulled out a switchblade knife and put it right on my stomach. He wanted the money. I told ditzo (Doris) to hand over the cash immediately and she said, "they are only joking." I told her if we lived through this I would kill her, and then she handed over the money and the boys ran down the stairs as fast as they could. I think it was their first "JOB" because they were as nervous as I was. I don't think they expected to see girls and it surprised them, which gave me time to get out of the elevator. There is nothing like the click and sight of a long, sharp, switchblade knife.

We then had to go down to the janitor for the building to tell her to lock the doors so people like this couldn't get in. The janitor's daughter was the girl Huey had gone with for awhile. You can imagine how humiliating this was for me as she was home and I felt like a real jerk. Her mother told us we would have to report it to the police. When we left I said to Doris, "Strike One." She doesn't want to be bothered.

We then walked a half block to the 42nd Police Station to tell our tale of woe to somebody. In charge of the desk was a great big cop and he was looking at us as If we were crazy. The last thought on his mind was writing up a report for $16.00. He told us if we saw these boys again to let him know. When we left I said to Doris, "STRIKE TWO!" Did he expect us to hog tie them and drag them back to the station house?

Now it was time to face the Green Grocer, who accused us of setting up the whole thing. By now I was furious. I was almost knifed and nobody cared. The idiot wanted his groceries (which we were still dragging around) and his money. I said rather loudly, "Do I sound like a Puerto Rican boy to you? Do you honestly think we would go through all this to split $16.00 five ways?" I was hoping Daddy wouldn't come out of the house because that would be disastrous, as he would never let anyone bully us. But, Mrs. Bissonnette lived in the front apartment and we lived behind her. She heard him yelling at us and calling us thieves and went to tell my father. I looked over at our stoop, and there he was looking very stern! He came right over and wanted to know what was going on. The stupid Green Grocer told my father we stole his money. I thought Daddy was going to kill him or at least lay him flat on the ground. I expected to see watermelons and all sorts of groceries flying around the store. He grabbed him by his white jacket and told him if he ever heard anyone talking about this incident he would be back and all his produce would be on the sidewalk with the owner on top of it. He then threw his bags of groceries at him.

We walked back across the street and it was our turn. "How many times have I told you?" We have all heard the rest I am sure.

WALTON HIGH SCHOOL STRIKE

I was probably in my junior year at Walton High School when many of us decided to go out on strike. This was a huge school and the very best in the Bronx. Daddy chose it for me. Most of the girls were Jewish and lived on the Grand Concourse. The Jews were very adamant that all their children, boys and girls, get a good education. We were all sent to that school because it was the best.

However, there was one teacher no one liked. She wasn't a good teacher and we wanted to get her out of our school. We had a very difficult State Regent's exam to pass before we could graduate and she wasn't helping at all. We took it up with the principal, but she was of course on the teacher's side. We decided to all go out on strike. We had two lunch periods. We made plans during the first period and then it was passed along to the next. It was all very exciting. We even decided to have a uniform. I can't believe I did all this, knowing Daddy's view of the respect we must have for our school. It almost felt like we were planning a prison break or some kind of espionage.

We all had a plain white blouse with a black skirt, which my mother made for me, not knowing what I was using it for. We wore black nylons and black shoes. In Italy, they introduced a line of shoes called "Capezios." I don't know how to spell it. But it was like a ballet shoe and everyone had a pair. Of course we could not afford the real ones, but Miles and National somehow copied them and sold them for about $5.00. We all felt so proud to be so organized, and we actually were very organized.

The minute I walked in the house after school, Daddy was waiting for me. He said, "Did you go on strike at school today?" OH NO! I thought I was so clever and pulled it off very nicely. I asked how he knew and he said it was all over The Bronx Home News.

We made the front page of the newspaper and many pages inside. What could I say? There I was in my strike uniform. I grabbed the paper, but you really couldn't make out any faces. He didn't say much because he always told us to do what we believed in, and he wanted us to have good teachers. He just sort of shook his head and went to take a rest. We thought we were so clever, but we never realized it would make the paper. Nothing much was happening in the Bronx at that time so we were the best story they had in a long while and they gook advantage of it.

When I read over these stories, I think I sort of sound rebellious, but I wasn't. I was a very good girl, but somehow I was curious. However, things didn't seem to work out the way they should have. I really never wanted to do anything wrong and hurt my parents. I loved them so much.

NEVER, NEVER, NEVER, NEVER GET ON A MOTORCYCLE

Sometime soon after the war, Victor Winter decided he wanted to buy a motorcycle. It was the hit of the neighborhood, as no one had such a luxury. Buddy was pretty fascinated with it too. He always liked to try new things. So he got on and took a ride around the block. Then he asked Mary if she would like a ride. She too was game. Never mind helmets or licenses. This would just be a nice little ride around the block. He took her all over our area of the Bronx – all the way to Yankee Stadium, then down the Concourse to 149th Street and then all the way home. He then wanted Peggy to go, but she very wisely declined. I am glad I wasn't there because I trusted him and would have gone with him. This would have been a disaster for as he got to the end of the street, to make the turn, the bike wouldn't cooperate, and he was headed straight for the candy store window right in front of him. A boy was sitting under the window reading a comic book and this bike was coming right at him. Fortunately, Buddy somehow turned the bike on the side and hit the wall just below the window. He went flying off, but got off with few injuries. I didn't see it, as I was at a friend's house, but everyone in the area was in shock that he survived the crash. Huey was standing outside of Maldacher's and said it was horrible.

I came home just before 10:00 (my curfew) and stopped at the candy store for Daddy's evening paper. I met a friend of mine and she asked me how Buddy was. Was he in the hospital or jail? She explained (to my horror) what had happened. I flew across the street and ran in the house yelling, "Where is Buddy? Is he hurt? Is he in jail?" Everyone started telling me to be quiet because Daddy was in bed and he didn't know anything about it. Since he wasn't really hurt, the police didn't know either. He never got on another motorcycle again. I only found out recently that he was always telling his two children and their friends to never, never, never, never get on a motorcycle, but they never knew why, so I told them. One for you Buddy. I miss you so much, especially on the holidays when I remember how I would call you about how long to cook the roast beef and the corned beef. Now my son Dan and Danny Rozak call me each holiday for cooking instructions.

MRS. WATERS

Mrs. Waters and her family moved into our apartment building before the war. Her name was Cathleen and she was called Cal for short. She moved in with her widowed father, her brother, her sister, Josephine, her twelve year old son, Tommy and her little girl, Carol Anne. Her mother died on Christmas Eve and her husband on New Year's Eve. They both had pneumonia and died one week apart. We didn't have funeral homes at that time. So the person was waked at home. They hung up a huge black wreath on the front door of the apartment building so anyone passing by would know that someone had passed away. We always felt sad and said a prayer for the family. Very soon the people would move out of the apartment and into another, I guess to get a fresh start or perhaps they thought it would bring them bad luck to stay there. The Irish were very superstitious and no one ever explained it to me.

A wonderful relationship developed until we all moved out of the Bronx. My father knew Mrs. Waters' husband who was twelve years older than she was. They grew up together down in Manhattan and remained friends. We saw her all the time. She came to all our parties and visited often. Josephine was really nice and we were very friendly too. However, she was an enigma as she never revealed anything about her past or what was happening in her life at this time. I think her father may have been an Irish Born Tyrant. I remember twice during the war seeing her meet a soldier in front of our house. She didn't let him in the house. Anyway, she too was great fun.

Carol Anne was thrilled with us as she lived with all adults and needed someone to play with. Since she was at our house so often with her mother she became very attached. She copied everything we did and wanted to be just like us. One time Bootsie and I got two lovely flannel nightgowns from The Home Relief and Carol Anne told her mother she wanted one so badly. Mrs. Waters stopped in one day and asked my mother if she would please tell her where she could buy this nightgown. She didn't want to ask but was exhausted going to every store in the Bronx. My mother told her she was sorry she didn't come to her first as she would never find them in any store. She explained they came from The Home Relief, but she would make one for Carol Anne. She wrote down everything she would need and sent her off to the fabric store and Carol Anne had her nightgown in two days. She even slept at our house with us so we could all be like sisters.

Mrs. Waters started to work when Carol Anne started school. She left her in our house and we took her to school and then when she got home she stayed with us until her mother got home at 5 o'clock. She spent the whole summer with us when we had the bungalows and we drove her mother out to spend the weekends with us. She was the life of the party and needed that connection.

Soon after Mrs. Waters and clan moved in a recent widow named Mrs. Gleason moved into the building with her bachelor son and a daughter. People did not leave home until they married. If they did not marry they stayed home with their family. I don't know why today the kids all want to move out at 18. It was more fun to stay home and be around family.

Well Mrs. Gleason was a good friend of my mother's. She grew up with her in Manhattan and had seen her sometimes later in life. She was a fine woman, but was very quiet. We saw her, but not as often as Mrs. Waters. She was not a party girl. When the war broke out her big handsome Irish son joined the Army. He was full of fun and we all missed him as we did all the boys who went away. My mother knew Mrs. Gleason liked cherry pie and had me take one up to her. Her big round table was filled with souvenirs from Holland. She was so thrilled with this package that she had me try on the wooden shoes, the aprons and Dutch hat. I held all the lovely plates and pitchers. It was a wonderful time because it made her so happy.

The problems started soon after. Jimmie was sent to The Battle of The Bulge and he was never the same after that. He came home an alcoholic and never functioned normally again. Some nights he would come home and sleep under the stairs. My father would pull this big man up the three flights to his apartment. Many times his mother would come down and ask my father to help her get him home safe. This had to be devastating for this poor woman as she never wanted anyone to know and knew she could trust my father.

This has been the introduction for the thing that followed. The Gleasons lived in Apt. 3C and the Waters in 4C above them. Josephine and Cal slept in one big bed. One night Josephine asked her sister if she was in bed. Her sister said, "Yes of course. Why are you asking me that? You know we always sleep in the same place" Josephine said, "WELL WHO IS GETTIG IN ON MY SIDE OF THE BED? SOMEONE IS IN OUR BED AND HE SMELLS LIKE WHISKEY. WHAT ARE WE GOING TO DO??? DA WILL KILL HIM IF HE FINDS HIM!!! Cal decided it had to be Jimmy and they had to dress him in the dark and get him very quietly passed their Da's bedroom and out the front door. Then they had to very carefully get him down the flight of stairs without him falling and waking everyone up. They opened his door and pushed him in so his mother wouldn't know as she was a very private person and would never got over the humiliation.

The only people they told was our family. She didn't want anyone else to know for the family's sake. Even though we felt so bad about what had happened to this fine family we couldn't help but have a good laugh. You know, you couldn't make this stuff up!

EDWARD THOMAS LYNCH

This is our brother Eddie, remember the little weasel? But when he grew up he was the most generous and kind person you could ever have the pleasure of living with.

He was very handsome and all the girls loved him and were constantly calling him on the phone. My mother was upset because she could not believe a girl should ever phone a boy.

Eddie always liked to look like a hot shot and was very fussy about his clothes. He always looked great. He had a clothing account at a store called Prentice Hall on 150th Street and Melrose Avenue. After payday he would give my mother his payment book and money and my mother would go down and pay his account for him. It was just a little book where they wrote in your purchases and payments. He was very serious about his account and always wanted it up to date. One day I went with Mama. I didn't realize it was a store for both men and women. I noticed a lovely suit and mentioned it to my mother. She said "you are working now and you should have a nice suit to wear to work." She wanted me to buy it, but I said I didn't make enough money yet to afford it. She replied "Put it on Eddie's account, he won't care. You know how generous he is." I said "You can do that??" I guess you could, because we did and I went home with a maroon suit that I loved.

That night as we were finished with our dinner Eddie said "Mom can you get my book? I made some extra overtime this week and I want to make an extra payment on my account." I almost had a heart attack and Mama tried to talk him out of it by saying she was going down that way the next day and she would be happy to take care of it. He could see by the way we were acting something was not quite right. He said, "Okay, what is going on." So we had to fess up. He asked me what I was so nervous about and gave me permission to use his account anytime I wanted to, and just make sure I made the extra payments on time. I showed him the suit and he said I would look beautiful in it. So the next day I went back and bought another one.

One time I went shopping with Peggy at Macy's in Parkchester in the Bronx. She was probably buying material because she was always sewing something. I hated sewing and was more interested in the housewares department as I was engaged and was planning on getting married when Huey was discharged from the Army. I was slowly putting items away so we would be prepared. I saw a beautiful set of china that I fell in love with. I showed it to Peggy and she said, "why don't you buy it?" I replied that I could not afford it yet. So you can guess what happened next. She said "Put it on my account," and I went home with a beautiful set of china.

I thought it was a good thing that I took business math in High School as I would need it to keep my accounts up to date and I had better stop shopping with everyone.

Getting back to Eddie, one night in about 1952 I went with Huey's mother and brother to visit with his other brother. Peggy and Mama went out to Teaneck, New Jersey to visit Mary and Jack and planned on staying the night. Mary lived there for a short time before she moved to Minnesota. The others were married except for Eddie, and Daddy was in the hospital. Eddie thought I had gone to Mary's. I came home at about 11:00 to a completely dark and empty apartment. I was 20 years old and had never been alone in the apartment at night before and I was very frightened. As time went on I was sure someone would break into the place as the neighborhood was changing. By 1:00 I couldn't stand it anymore so I called Eddie at Ross's bar hoping that he was there. It was only two blocks away. The bartender said to Eddie," Eddie this is for you it's some hysterical girl." I am surprised he even came to the phone since he had so many girls after him. When he got on I started crying and telling him how I was home alone and was so frightened. He said "don't be afraid I will be right home." He came home and told me how sorry he was. He would not have gone out if he knew I was coming home. He told me to get ready for bed and made me a cup of tea. He promised me he wouldn't go out again so I could go to bed and not worry. How many brothers would do that for a sister? Most would have called me a big baby and hung up the phone. I don't even know if he was with a date. I am sure he was with friends, so much for "The Weasel." I miss him so much.

Mary was the first one to get married. My father was in the hospital at the time so Buddy was the father of the bride. He also got his band to play at the wedding, so he had a double role as did Garrity, who played in the band and was also the chauffeur. His family really did have a chauffer, so he borrowed the uniform and the limo.

OUR BABY SISTER

Florence Lynch was born twenty-two months after I was. She was the seventh of seven children and for some reason she was called Bootsie, and still is. The Lynch's loved nick-names and had many of them. Actually we had the least. Maybe that is why they got a little carried away with Bootsie.

She was the cutest little girl with real blonde hair and blue eyes. Everyone treated her like the baby and she was lots of fun.

Jimmie was born fifteen months before I was, so we were great friends, and we all played great together. When Jimmie started school, Bootsie and I started playing many games together. We were ages five and three. One of our favorite games to play was school. One Christmas, Santa brought us a children's table and two chairs. On each chair was a little Shirley Temple doll. We would each have a turn being the teacher and playing school. When it was my turn to be the teacher, I got to use the table. We would then take newspapers and cut them up into little rectangles and put them on the floor as the kids' desks.

We roller skated all the time, played paper dolls and really loved playing house with the doll carriage. We had one bike and we rode it up and down the block all the time. We had a friend in our building who had a relative who came to visit them. This man had a car and let us play house in it. It was like a cute little house with fancy shades to pull down over the windows. She always let us know as soon as he arrived so we could get our babies' bottles and blankets.

We even made our First Holy Communion together. Our parents were so proud and so were we. My mother made our dresses, and we had little white pocketbooks, our own Rosaries and prayer books. We sat next to each other in the church and went up together for our Communion. It felt like such a Holy Day to us.

The parents filed out first and then we followed. We each had the most beautiful white carnation bouquets which came from our Uncle Larpse, the Undertaker. We felt like two little brides. It was the tradition in the family to visit the Aunts and Uncles on special holidays and they always raved over us.

We had one terrible experience when we were just little girls. We were on our way home from church and two blocks from our house was a corner gas station which of course didn't have a curb so the cars could roll right in. As it happened, a sixteen year old flew up that space on his bike and knocked Bootsie down on her side. He then ran the tires over her face and took off. She was about six and I was about eight. I was horrified because she couldn't get up at first and was dazed. She still doesn't remember it to this day. I had two blocks to half carry her home. In the time it took to get her home, the one side of her face was completely swollen, black and blue and she had a totally closed eye. I didn't know if she even had an eye.

My father's brother, Uncle Eddie, showed up during the early morning and was sitting in my mother's chair talking to him when I came crying in with this mess. My poor father was so upset because he thought maybe she did lose her eye. Poor Uncle Eddie had a hangover and went into the bathroom and got sick. He asked Daddy if he could do anything at all to help, but Daddy was going to take her to the ER. Mama was already packing ice on her. Any way, Uncle Eddie decided to go home. He said, "Nellie will be very angry, but nothing she says could be as bad as this." He came back the next day to see how things were. That would teach him to visit us unannounced again.

HAPPILY EVER AFTER

I was preparing to graduate in January. Whenever we had parties or any kind of activity I used to ask Doris to have her boyfriend Andy pass it on to Huey, but he never came. It seems he just wanted to play ball. We would go ice skating, roller skating, to the movies and to all the dances we could find. He never attended he just wanted to play ball all day and he worked for the post office at night.

I did notice during that month that he paid a little bit more attention to me. He actually went sleigh riding one night and asked me to ride with him. I almost fainted. He walked all the way home with me and talked all the way. When we stopped for hot chocolate at the ice-cream parlor he paid some attention to me. I guess mostly teasing, but I knew things were changing.

On Christmas night. I asked my mother if I could have some friends in for a party, playing records and having some refreshments. She said I could but I would have to be in charge. Doris asked Andy to let Huey know. We didn't know if he would come, but miracle of miracles he walked in the door. He immediately told me he had to leave at 10:00 as he had to be up at five to deliver the mail. I said that was fine and I understood. Well he actually danced every dance with me and we sat and talked all night. He didn't leave until 11:00 and he really had to force himself to leave then. I walked him to the door and thanked him for coming and he said he had a wonderful time. I said goodnight and looked in his eyes and knew he was mine. After four long years the angels were smiling down on me.

We were all invited to a New Year's Eve party at another girl's house and he came to that one also. He never let me out of his sight. He stayed right next to me. He did not have to leave early because of the holiday. We stayed quite late and had a wonderful time. When it was time for me to go home he walked me home and we sat on the stoop for a little while. I was very happy Daddy wasn't sitting outside this time because I didn't need any help and knew just what to do.

We met when I was a freshman and he came to my graduation. I didn't know he was there until I was walking up the aisle after receiving my diploma. I was so happy. As they say: "The rest is history."

HUEY'S STORY

It was the fall of 1945 when I met Dena. My friend Larry took me over to Elton Avenue and 160th Street, where he played ball with a bunch of his friends. He introduced me to the guys and there were some girls our age (fourteen) there.

Dena told me years later that my back was to her that day and when I turned around she saw my face and she suddenly blurted out to her close friend, Doris, that she was going to marry that boy someday, whoever he was. She said it was such a strong feeling, as though she had known me in another life.

I had no such feeling toward her. Dena wore an awful looking green overcoat all winter that went down below her knees and buttoned right up to her neck. It turned me off every time I saw her walk by.

People tried many times to interest me in going to dances or parties or to go roller skating, but I had no interest in those things. All I wanted to do was play baseball, preferably for the Yankees.

Over the next three or four years we went out on group dates to Jones Beach or to Coney Island or boat rides up the Hudson, but I really had no strong feelings towards any of the girls until one night Dena invited me to a Christmas party at her home. She must have been shocked when I told her I would like to come.

The night of the party I saw Dena really for the first time. She was wearing a very nice white blouse and black velvet skirt, and looked so pretty, I was immediately attracted to her. We spent a wonderful evening dancing and talking and she told me all about her family of three brothers and three sisters. Dena was the sixth of seven children. I saw how much she loved her mother and father and learned how hard she worked to help them in keeping their home a clean and happy place. She did the washing, ironing, cleaned every room in their apartment and even painted when that was needed.

This was a young lady with character, full of love for her parents and family, smart and a wonderful personality. It was a pleasure to talk with her and share her thoughts.

That night changed everything for me. We began going on dates and I was falling in love with this pretty young lady who some people said looked a lot like Jacqueline Kennedy.

I continued with the post office and was happy to be able to give my parents some help after their interminable struggle which had been going on for over twenty years.

1950 brought more Communist aggression, this time in Korea. The draft was started again and many young men from our neighborhood began leaving for the induction centers. A few days before my 21st birthday I received my draft notice. I was to report for duty the day after my birthday on October 9, 1951.

It was a sad day all the way around, especially to have to leave my family and Dena when we had been talking about getting married. But this was serious business. By the end of 1951 we were losing a lot of wonderful young men in a terrible battle where a fanatical enemy had to be stopped.

Christmas was a few days off and I was able to get home for a few days. I was held at the camp until it was almost too late to catch the last train out from Baltimore to New York to make it home before Christmas. A buddy of mine from New York and I raced to the taxi stand at the gate and told the driver we would give him a ten dollar tip if he could get us to Baltimore in time to catch that last train to New York.

I'll never forget that ride. We hit 100 miles an hour and we were airborne on some of those highway straightaways. We barely made the train.

I had a wonderful time at home for Christmas. I bought an engagement ring and gave it to Dena as a Christmas present. She said it was the happiest day of her life after all those years she spent hoping I would take notice of her.

I passed the machinist course I had been taking and envisioned myself running a lathe or milling machine in Seoul for the next year or so.

Then some great news came after we graduated from the school. I was being sent to Fort Belvoir in Virginia to be assigned to France for the remainder of my two years. What a relief!

It was now April of 1952 and I was to spend two weeks in Belvoir getting shots and preparing for the boat trip across the Atlantic. I would get some time off before I would leave for Europe.

I came home in April and Dena and I talked about marriage, but we decided to wait. If I had to do it over again, I think we should have married then. We had a wonderful time together and soon it was time to leave again. This time I could not come home for about 18 months. Dena came to the train station with me and then I realized we should have married. It was very sad for us both. I promised to write often and then I had to board the train and wave goodbye.

1951-1952-1953

1951 was a very happy year for me. Huey and I were dating seriously for one and one half years. That summer we decided to start making plans to get married. We were only 19 and 20 years old so we had quite a time putting away enough money to buy a car, buy some furniture and get an apartment we could afford.

The only thing I had to be sad about was that my father contracted tuberculosis in 1949. His brother died from it a short time before and Daddy was visiting him right to the day he died. He must have picked up the germ at that time. He was not very ill and was able to come home when allowed. It was a terrible disease and most people died from it because they did not have any medication to treat them. We visited him often while he was in the hospital.

At the same time we were at war with Korea. I was so involved in my own life that I wasn't even aware of it until Huey got his draft notice at the end of September. I was heart broken to think he would have to go to war. We had just finished with a war in Europe and Japan. He reported for two year's duty in the US Army. He came home for two week furlough at Christmas and gave me a beautiful engagement ring. I was so happy! We decided to wait until he came home in two years to get married because we wouldn't be together anyway and his family needed the money from his allotment from the army.

Huey came home again in late May for a two week furlough and then he was headed for France for fifteen months. I thought I would never make it when I went to Penn Station to see him off. It was just terrible. I cried so hard waving goodbye to him while he, in his uniform, waved out the open window of the train. I waited until the train was out of sight and then cried all the way home on the subway. I felt like I was living in one of the old movies from World War II. I never dreamed I would have to go through this.

However, life goes on. I had a wonderful job at General Electric that I loved. I was a statistical typist and was making a good salary. Every payday I put as much as I could in a bank account which was growing nicely for the day Huey came home.

I didn't realize it, but I had some big changes that were coming my way. I would have opportunities to help others and that would make me happier. I also was going to have my whole world crash down around me that December at age 21.

I used to take the New York Central to work every morning as it was a nicer ride that the subway and was only about four blocks from my house. One morning in early June as I turned the corner of 161st Street I noticed a little brown house between two apartment buildings. It was old and had a wrought iron gate in front with two patches of grass on each side of the stone steps to the front door. I don't know why I never noticed it before as I passed there everyday. But, this time there was an old man sitting in the window just gazing out. He looked lonely so I waved to him. His whole face lit up. I could not believe that one simple wave could make someone so happy. I decided I would go past his house every morning just in case he was there again. The next morning I was shocked to see him standing at the gate. He was paralyzed on one side and could not speak. I went up to him and took his hand and spoke to him telling him about myself. I was choking back the tears as I didn't want him to think I felt sorry for him but that I was his friend. I told him I would come by every morning at this same time. I was also surprised how doing such a small thing for someone could make me feel so happy. Every morning he was at that gate. I don't know how he got there because there wasn't anyway to get down the steps unless someone else lived there and took him out. I started to leave cookies Mama made or some homemade bread. There were times I brought him a jar of homemade soup. Whatever I could think of that would help him. One chilly October morning he was in an old sweater with holes in the elbows. The next day I brought him a sweater I had gotten my father and he hadn't had a chance to wear it yet. My friend was thrilled and wore it every morning until winter. He did have a warm jacket. I looked forward to seeing him every day and it made me forget some of my own sadness with Huey gone for so long.

In early December I came down with a terrible cold. The doctor gave me penicillin and told me to come back in two weeks if I wasn't feeling much better and to stay quiet and not leave the house. I returned to him and he took an x-ray and told me I had pneumonia and had to be hospitalized. I went to St. Francis Hospital in the South Bronx. I remember I was the only one in a room with about ten beds. It was rather lonely, but my bed was by the window and I could watch all the people running around doing Christmas shopping. I spent my birthday there on December 18th, and the next day my doctor came in and told me I had tuberculosis. It was a compete shock to me and I was about hysterical. The TB Hospital was right across the street and he wanted to bundle me up and wheel me across. I absolutely refused. I just couldn't even think straight, but I absolutely was not going into any TB Hospital. I signed myself out of the hospital and went home. The doctor later told my mother that telling me I had TB was one of the worst things he ever had to do.

I decided to get a second opinion and went to a hospital on the Grand Concourse where my father's doctor was. This time they told me they did not find the germ. You can imagine how elated I was, but there was also that little doubt in the back of my mind. Then a nice young priest came in to visit me. We chatted and had a nice time until he saw my ring. He said, "I see you have a very fine ring. I am sure you are marrying a fine young Irish Catholic lad." I said, "He is a very fine lad, but he is German and Lutheran." The room immediately turned to ice. I thought here it comes. He told me I must marry in the Catholic Church and that Huey should change his religion. I said that now that I was sick things were a little different and I had nine months to think about it. I was concerned about having children. He said if we were to marry in the Catholic Church we could not be allowed inside the Altar Rail and they would not bless the ring. I told him I thought that was very insulting and not very Christian. He told me if I married outside the Catholic Church I would be doomed to eternity and then he walked out. The same thing happened to me with the priest in the TB hospital.

I went home and continued to get sicker. I decided I would try one more hospital because I did not want to accept the fact that I was a very sick young woman. I went to Morrisania Hospital in the Bronx. They put me in a very large ward with about fifty beds. One section which was a separate alcove was for the women with TB, but it was filled. The women were very nice to me and came to keep me company. When anyone came to see me from outside they had to wear all white. It felt like a meeting with the KKK. I still did not want to accept that I was so sick. I mentioned to one of the ladies that I had a chance to get into St. Joseph's Hospital. She said if there was a chance to get in to do it because she had been a patient there and was treated very well. She decided to leave on her own and when she was sick again they didn't have any beds. I called my mother and asked her to check with the doctor and he got a bed for me. I think maybe he was saving it for me because he knew I could never get better on my own. My mother and Jimmie drove me right down.

I was put in a room with four older ladies who were very nice to me. I remember when lights were out and we were to go to sleep, I had to sleep with the head of the bed partly up because I coughed too much if I laid down. My ribs were very sore from coughing. I lay there and it was so quiet and I was in great despair because I knew this was not a two week stay. It could possibly go on for two or more years. Then someone coughed and it felt as though it sailed out her window and flew in mine. I will never forget that sound. I asked God to please help me and wondered what was going to happen to me. I was put on bed rest for three months except to use the bathroom which was right in my room. I was very unhappy and very frightened.

I still would not admit that I had TB and every night for one month I prayed that the next morning the doctor would come in and say it was all a mistake and I could go home. One night though I changed my prayer. I prayed that God would help me get better. I said I had waited too long and if he could just show me that He was there for me I would do everything and anything; even stay there until the doctors said I could be discharged in good health. I hadn't eaten hardly anything at all for one month. The Italian woman who served us breakfast would yell at me every morning because I would make her take the tray away. She would say "You so skinny, you gonna die if you don't eat." I couldn't even look at the food.

The next morning when I took the tray from her she was ecstatic. On the tray was a box of cereal, two soft boiled eggs, a piece of toast, a glass of orange juice and a pot of tea and I ate every bit of it! When she came back she practically fainted. I then asked her if I could have another tray just the same. I ate all of that also and did so until I gained 25lbs. I think I finally realized I could not get better unless I admitted to myself that I had TB and would surely die if I didn't stop feeling sorry for myself and did something about it. Of course I got better every week and soon Easter came and I was given the day off to go home. I wrote about that on another page at the end of this story. I asked my mother to go and visit my friend in the little brown house to tell him why I was no longer stopping to see him.

I was fortunate that General Electric paid me two thirds of my pay for six months. I told my mother to take what she needed for the house as I had been contributing to the expenses and to put the rest in my bank account. They also paid for my medical expenses. In New York City you did not have to pay for TB care, the city wanted you in the hospital, and not out spreading the disease, because it is an airborne disease. I guess they were so happy to have the people in the hospital the city paid for it. But, it was nice to know I was not a charity patient.

In about 1950 or so Tetracycline and a pill called PAS was discovered to treat TB patients and it saved many lives including mine. I got three injections three times a week and PAS every day. I am so grateful for the brave people who worked there. They were very kind and took excellent care of us.

One day I walked into the solarium and saw an old lady sitting in a wheel chair all by herself. I went over to her and we talked about our families. Her name was Florence Larkin and she was terribly crippled by arthritis. She was born in this country, but had many stories about Ireland told to her by her mother. I wish I could remember them now.

I made many friends young and old, but she became a special friend. My mother used to send my brother Jimmie down to me on Thursday nights with my favorite meal – two lamb chops, a baked potato and green beans. I would cut them up real small and feed them to Florence. She was so thrilled to have this delicious meal to look forward to. Florence was there about four months when they decided she did not have TB. They never found the germ on her. Her bones were so bent that it made shadows on her lungs. So she was discharged from the hospital and was very happy to go home. I was so happy for her but knew I would miss her. We had a nice garden on the main floor surrounded by a wrought iron fence and a small gate. We were only permitted into this garden at certain times which were very rare. They allowed me to wheel her down to the garden where her brother was waiting with his car. We both wept and I kissed her goodbye. When I returned, the doctor asked me if I had a choice between going home myself or seeing Florence go home what would I do. I said I would let Florence go, but only Florence, everyone else was on her own. I'd never let them out ahead of me.

One more sad story and that is all. Many of the Irish women who came to this country worked in the TB hospitals because there was no other work for them and most people would not take a job there because they were so afraid of the disease. We had several women who took care of us and lived in the convent just like the nuns. Some of them may even have had to devote some time to the hospital because the hospital sponsored them. I am sure they were desperate for help. So, we had some women who stayed because it was security for them. One woman who worked in the laundry came here with her husband and baby. The baby died and he left her all alone. She came to work at St. Joseph's as a very young girl and you can imagine how hard it was to do all that laundry with out the convenient equipment we have today. She found she had cancer and was very ill. They put her in a room on our floor and just waited for her to die. The time came very shortly and on the last night they put her in a room next to the doctor's and nurses' office. We did not have a nurse or doctor on duty at night. A nun would make periodic checks on everyone during the night. It really bothered me that this woman was going to die alone. I thought she had such a hard life that someone should be with her at least at the end. So, after lights out, I went down to her room and stayed with her. I went and got a rocking chair and pulled the curtain around her bed. The nun did find me on her inspections, but allowed me to stay there which was kind of shocking. I rocked all night and said prayers for her. The next morning when the nurse and doctor came in they were not too happy that I had stayed up all night, but I was getting near time to go home. I told them I did not want her to be alone. They told me to go to bed and they would be with her as they were now on duty. About twenty minutes later they came to tell me she had passed away soon after I left. I wanted to be with her at the time she passed away, but was satisfied that the doctor was there and she did not die alone.

The only reason I tell these stories is because when my posterity reads this I want them to know that it is sometimes very simple to make someone happy. Just a wave can change a person's life or making friends with someone who doesn't really have friends can make them so happy if you take an interest in them. I think I have always been drawn to people. I was very interested in those around me. The more you help others the happier you will be. Somehow it rubs off on you and makes you forget your own troubles and really look forward to making friends.

Many people ask me what I did for a whole year in a hospital. We had a library for those who could leave their rooms and a mobile one for those who could not, so I did a lot of reading. I was taught by some kind ladies how to crochet and knit which I loved. I even made hot pads on a special loom. Making the hot pads made me a little uncomfortable because it made me think of people in mental institutions. Actually they were very strong and I used them for years, but I drew the line at basket weaving! Buddy and Joan were living in Texas at the time and sent me some argyle socks to knit. I had the most wonderful time with all those little spools that hung down with the different colors for socks. There were gray socks with red, yellow and black wool and brown ones with yellow, green and blue. I learned how to turn the heel and to taper the toe. I also learned to make mittens for Danny Rozak, my nephew who lived with us and was someone I loved very much. So, if you have a good attitude which takes awhile to acquire, you learn to be happy and adjust and be grateful for the people who discovered the medicine that kept you alive.

I was discharged in time for Thanksgiving in 1953. You can imagine my joy at going home. Huey came home from the Army in September 1953. It was difficult to be in the hospital while he was home, but I promised myself I would not leave until I was discharged by the doctors. I felt I had a right to live a normal like if I was completely free of the disease and I was proud of myself for sticking it out. I looked for my friend in the old brown house, but he was gone and no one seemed to know where he was, so I just couldn't find him.

The doctor told us to wait six months to get married, two years to start a family and to have only two children. Well we got two of them right anyway. We were married in May of 1954 and even though we have had our heartaches and joys I feel we have been blessed for these 56 years and hope we have many more. We love each other just as much as we did back in 1950 and that is a great blessing.

EASTER SUNDAY 1953

I was in the TB Hospital three months when I was allowed to go home for the Easter Holiday. I had been sick for four months, but refused to enter the hospital until I knew I had to. It was very difficult because I truly loved our home and knew I would be so lonely.

I was very excited to finally have a day off outside of the hospital. Jimmie picked me up with his car and drove me back that night. He was so good to me, always bringing letters and packages from home to keep me happy. Huey's mother begged me not to tell Huey I was sick while he was in the Army in France. Huey wrote everyday as did I, but the mail went to our house and Jimmie made many trips in the evening to bring them to me.

Daddy was in another hospital and my doctor made me promise I would not make the trip to see him as it was quite a distance. Daddy was very worried about me and wanted us to be sure to take pictures. When the pictures came back I realized I wasn't smiling on any of them. As much as I loved the day at home I knew I would have to return to the hospital as I had promised myself I would not leave until I was officially declared TB free and in good health. So I was sad at the thought of the day ending.

I decided that I had much to be grateful for as I was getting better all the time so I made myself learn to smile. It was very difficult as I guess my brain was telling me not to. I would look in the mirror many times a day to force myself to smile. At first I actually had to pull my lips to loosen up my mouth. However, I was determined and after a short time I could smile on my own. I still had to use the mirror to remind me how important this really was to my well being. Pretty soon I was smiling all the time and was a very grateful young lady.

HOME FOR THE FOURTH OF JULY

The next time I was permitted to have a day home was July 4th. This time, however, I didn't want to be picked up. I wanted to go home on my own and feel the sidewalk beneath my feet and walk among the regular people bustling along the street. I wanted to feel free and to prove to myself I could do it after so many months inside. I had to walk a couple of blocks to the first bus on 149th Street where I would transfer to the bus that would take me home. I walked around a little while enjoying all the excitement. This area seemed like a hub of the Bronx. You could see the Third Avenue El, the subway was right on the corner, there were many stores and three movies right by. I wanted to go in the stores, but didn't want to worry my mother and was so anxious to get home. A Chinese Restaurant was right on the corner and the smells were flowing out of the door. Doris and I used to go there when we could and loved the delicious food and the ambiance was so mysterious to us.

When I got off the bus many of my neighbors were out on the street or looking out of their apartment windows. They all called and waved to me expressing their pleasure at seeing me looking so healthy. My mother had made me a pretty plaid cotton skirt and a peasant blouse which had black ribbon inserted in the sleeves and the neck. I felt like a million dollars. I spent the day with my family and a few of my friends and it was wonderful.

It wasn't as difficult to return at night as I knew I was doing really well and the time was coming when I would be going home for good. I had Jimmie drive me back as I wanted to wait until the last minute.

I was discharged just a few days before Thanksgiving. As soon as I got home I wanted to see Daddy. I hadn't seen him since Christmas and I really missed him. Buddy drove me out to Long Island where Daddy was and what a glorious reunion it was. He was so happy I was well. He was devastated when I got sick as he knew it came from him. He got TB from his brother, our Uncle Larpse, who died at age 47 and Daddy used to visit him all the time.

I would do it all again as I enjoyed my visits with Daddy and wanted to see as much of him as I could while he was still alive. I learned from this experience that I was a much stronger person than I thought I was. I also learned that it is not so much what happens to you in life it is how you handle it. I was a lot different than the girl who cried because she was alone in the empty apartment.

MATCHMAKER, MATCHMAKER MAKE ME A MATCH

The year was 1952 and all the young men in the neighborhood had been drafted for the Korean War. We girls had all graduated and had gone our own way. Doris joined the WACS so she was gone too. I had a group of friends that would meet for dinner or attend movies. Agnes Parker was a friend who lived right across the street. She was an only child so she started coming to our apartment to visit me. She noticed that Peggy loved to sew and asked her if she would mind teaching her how to sew. She pretty much became Peggy's friend and had a great time making clothes.

Bill Kiley was her uncle and I had known him for years and years. He lived in the same apartment house as Agnes. We always referred to him as Uncle Bill, not to his face of course as we were a little afraid of him, he seemed kind of grouchy to us. Looking back I can understand as we were always spread out all over the stoop when he came home from work and he would have to climb over all of us just to get into the house. We would only move about enough for him to get one foot on the step, so he had that to look forward to every night. I remember when he would come home from World War II on furlough. HE would look so handsome in his Captain's Uniform. We would politely say "Hello, Mr. Kiley."

One evening Agnes and I went to the ice-cream parlor for a treat and while we were talking she said "What do you think about matching Peggy and Uncle Bill?" I replied "AGNES WHERE HAVE WE BEEN ALL THESE YEARS!!! WERE WE BRAIN DEAD? THEY LIVED RIGHT ACROSS FROM EACH OTHER AND WE NEVER THOUGHT TO INTRODUCE THEM!!!! THEY EVEN GO TO THE SAME MASS EVERY SUNDAY! THEY ARE A PERFECT MATCH!" When I calmed down I asked how we were going to arrange it.

Agnes's mother was Bill's sister and she was making some drapes for her windows so we asked Peggy if she would be kind enough to go to her house and help her. Peggy agreed and somehow Agnes got Bill on some pretense to come up to their apartment. The Match was made. We were so proud, but wondered if they would be interested in each other.

The next Sunday Peggy was sitting in her pew at church and Bill came along and asked would she mind if he sat with her. He then asked her to a Yankee game.

Years later when Peggy was visiting here she was telling this story to my girls and Carol said "You should have said PARK IT, BABY." We all howled laughing because that would have been the end of that romance. Bill probably would have run for the door and had to find a new church to attend! Peggy was actually one of Agnes's bridesmaids. I wasn't even considered. Well, the rest is history.

PEGGY'S COAT

Peggy owned a coat that I coveted for a long time, but I knew she loved it and was not about to part with it. Well along came Bill and he hated the coat so guess who got her hot little hands on it? I thought I could rule New York City and that I was a really hot number in that coat.

When Daddy was in Bellevue's TB Wing I used to visit him all the time and many times I would stop at our local liquor store and pick up a pint of whiskey for him. I don't know what the store owner thought as I strutted out of his store with my head held high and my long curly Irish hair hanging down my back with whiskey in my pocketbook. He either thought I was an alcoholic or he knew exactly where I was heading. I often wondered what the nurses thought when I came in and Daddy had probably been a grouch all day and by the time I left he was happy and calm. I would sneak him a sip and before I left I would hide the bottle in the back of his drawer. I wondered what would happen to me if I ever got caught because surely they could smell it on his breath. But I was strong Irish and could handle anything. Little did I know until I was in the hospital that this went on all the time even with the women. One day the nurse told me the doctor would like to speak with me. I thought surely I was on my way to jail and would be banned from ever coming into that hospital again. But all he wanted was to warn me that I was spending a lot of time in this place and was at the perfect age for contracting TB. I told him I loved my father and wanted to see him as much as I could because we never knew what would happen to him. Of course he was right but that's another story. I will say that many times Daddy behaved himself and I stopped at a corner store at 28th street and First Avenue to get him coffee and buns. I loved the river behind the hospital and the big well lit avenue. I found it very exciting.

Well when I was leaving for Peggy's wedding, the ladies in my room asked me if I could ask my sister for a bottle of whiskey to bring back to them. I didn't drink, but it was done all the time. I replied I wouldn't have to ask my own sister. There would be bottles on all the tables and I would just take one. These were quart bottles not so easy to hide. But, I knew I could find a way. Huey wasn't so sure and was very nervous about the whole operation. He wanted to know how I was going to hide this bottle from everyone. I said "Don't worry, when we get to the hospital I will take my coat off and keep the neck of the bottle under my coat." We pressed the elevator button and when the doors opened the elevator was filled with nuns. They had some kind of retreat that weekend and were all over the place. They insisted we get on the elevator while I told them we would be happy to wait for the next one. They were so sweet and happy that I got on and made Huey stand in front of me so no one could brush up against my arm. As a matter of fact, they were so cheerful that I wondered if they had a wee bit of the communion wine at their meeting. They certainly weren't anything like the nuns I had in school. After lights were out I slept while a fine party was taking place and everyone was happy.

I told you I could manage anything in my magic coat. Of course it helped to be a little bit Irish. Who else would have the Chutzpah.

POTS AND PANS

While I was waiting for Huey to return from the war I was putting away various household items we could use when we got married. By this time I was working for General Electric and was making a nice salary so I did not have to put anything on anyone else's account. Peggy was just starting to go with Bill and was thinking along the same lines. One night while I was watching TV I saw an ad for pots and pans. I thought they looked like a great buy because there was a whole set with two extra pots with covers. So I called to Peggy and told her to look at this ad. Well, we both ordered the pots. We were very happy with them except I had the two pots with the covers and she had just the two pots and no covers. So I very generously gave her one of my covers. Peggy and Bill lived in the same apartment complex that Huey and I did. Actually I was the one who found this apartment for them. Huey and I had moved into a really nice place and Peggy was expecting Marybeth and needed more room. I spoke to the janitor and he had them come to look at it. It wasn't easy to get apartments at that time. So they took it right away and moved right in. Many times on my way home I would stop in to see Peggy and we would have a nice little chat. This one time it wasn't very pleasant as Peggy informed me that Bill hated the pots. (I am actually laughing as I write this.)

This is how the conversation continued:

Peggy: Remember those pots we bought, well Bill doesn't like them and he asked me where I bought them. I told him that Dena saw them on television and we each bought a set. He was somehow annoyed with having only one cover. He told Peggy he expected this from Dena, but thought Peggy had more sense.

Dena: Wait a minute here. Let's go back a little bit. What does he think I'm some kind of an idiot? Peggy started to get a little nervous realizing what she had just said.

Peggy: Well no he just always though you and your friends were very silly.

Dena: Of course we were silly, we were just teenagers and he was an old man at least fifteen years older than we were. Does he do any of the cooking?

Peggy: Of course he never has to cook anything. I do all the cooking.

Dena: Then tell him to mind his own business and stay out of the kitchen altogether and that he is not getting my pot cover. Remind him if it weren't for me he would still be living with his mother and I'd like to hear him complain about her pots. She's hit him with one. Agnes and I arranged to have him meet the girl of his dreams, and also I found this apartment you are living in.

We both burst out laughing. We had to hold our sides we were laughing so hard. I said "I can just see you telling Bill to mind his own business."

Just then little Billy came out of his bedroom from his nap and wanted to know what we were laughing about. I whispered to Peggy "Don't tell him. He is way too smart. Bill won't be in the door two minutes and he will tell him that Aunt Dena said he should mind his own business. I'll never get in the door again." The whole thing was hilarious and we have laughed about it many times over the years.

OUR LITTLE ANGEL

Our third child was born July 11, 1960 in New Jersey and we decided to call her Christine Mary Hilgenberg. We did not have the blessing of keeping her very long and for some reason when she was born I knew we would not be able to keep her and it terrified me. I suppose it was that old Irish intuition that was strong in me. It reminded me of when Mama had meningitis and I knew she would live. I was no longer a child now and I did not have the faith that I needed to completely trust her to God.

The day after she was born I asked the doctor if I could go home as Huey always took vacation time when I was having a baby. My mother stayed at our garden apartment in New Jersey to help him out and to watch over the children while he visited me at the hospital. I felt great and the baby was fine. They kept you in the hospital for four days for a normal birth. The doctor said he knew I was fine, but he liked to keep the babies four days because usually in that time he could tell if she had any problems. He then told me he had a mother who was doing really well so he let her go home and her baby died. I thought I was going to have a heart attack. This terrible feeling came over me and I could hardly breathe. I felt as thought someone was sitting on my chest. It was then that I knew she would leave us early. I wanted to tell Huey, but I knew I frightened him with my intuition and I could not even voice the feelings I had.

I was home a few days when I left the apartment to go out in the back yard where they had a play ground and lines for the wet wash. When I came back to the front steps a few ladies were gathered and I stopped to speak with them for a few minutes. I asked what they were talking about and they said they had a friend across the courtyard whose baby died in its sleep. The same feeling came over me and I could hardly breathe. I had to get away from them and went into the house.

Chrissy was the most beautiful baby. I did notice that she often looked over my shoulder and acted as though she recognized someone. She always laughed and cooed when she did this and she was not looking at me. I believe the people she left behind were visiting with her.

When people saw Chrissy they would always say how beautiful she was and that she looked just like an angel. Instead of being happy that everyone saw this in her I was so frightened. I didn't want anyone to see her as an angel. I just wanted my baby.

One day in early December, she suddenly stared crying very hard which she never did. I took her temperature and it was 104 degrees. I called the doctor. He was away, but a pediatrician was on call and came to the house. He said she had bronchitis and needed medicine and plenty of fluids. It seemed that I could not calm her down. Sunday afternoon she became lethargic so early the next morning I called my doctor and he came right over. As soon as he saw here he told me she was very sick and probably had staph pneumonia. Lori and Huey had both had staph infections for quite some time. They had a vaccine made that cured them. Little did I know they were growing inside of her. He told me she must get right to the hospital. I said I would call a taxi immediately, but he wanted to drive me to the hospital himself as he was very concerned. He made a call to the hospital and as soon as we got off the elevator a nurse was standing there and she grabbed Chrissy right out of my arms. That was the last time I got to touch her as she was in isolation. I called Huey and he came right home from work. All we could do was to look at her through a glass window. It was horrible. I wanted to go in and pick her up and hold her. This went on for ten days without any hope. One night Mama and I were sitting in the living room and someone knocked three hard distinctive knocks on my front door. I looked at Mama and I told her I wondered who it could be so late at night. Huey had already gone to bed. I went down and opened the door and no one was there. We were having a blizzard and there were no footsteps in the snow. I looked all around and finally closed the door. When I came up stairs I asked Mama if she had heard the knocks and she told me she hadn't, but I was sure she had by the expression on her face. I didn't know it but Mama told me later she had heard the knocks. She just didn't have the heart to tell me that the Irish believed that if someone in the house was going to die the angels come to warn you by knocking on the door three times.

On December 17th, I was at the hospital and the doctor said we were still not out of the woods, but when I left they were going to take her oxygen mask off to see how she did. I arrived home a little after 4 and as soon as I walked in the door the telephone rang. It was the doctor telling me how sorry he was, to have to tell me that Chrissy had passed away at 4. All hope was now gone.

We were devastated and I knew I had to hold myself together because I was three months pregnant with Patty. We actually had to face the horror of choosing a little white casket and burial clothes. I had a Jewish friend across the courtyard from us and she asked me to please use her daughter's dress she had from some Jewish ceremony. The dress would never be worn again and she would be so happy if I would use it. It was gorgeous, all white with pink ribbons down the front. It was Dec 17th, and I had done a little bit of shopping the night before for the children. I had bought Chrissy a little soft kitten and puppy which I put in her arms in the casket. I couldn't stand the thought of her being in there alone. We had a wake for one night. I had to see her again, touch her once more and prove to myself that she was really gone.

The next day was the funeral. We walked to the gravesite and they put her down in the open grave. Today they don't do that until everyone has left. But, we had to look down at the white casket six feet in the ground. I didn't want to leave her there. I waked away towards the car a few times, but had to go back to the gravesite and look down again. Everyone waited patiently for me to get the courage to finally leave. I wondered how I would ever go on living a normal life again.

My brother Buddy went home with us and stayed with my mother while we took Lori and Danny out to buy a Christmas tree. For their sakes I felt we had to be as normal as possible. We then spent a couple of nights purchasing toys for the other children. I don't remember much about that Christmas. Joan and Buddy came by with toys for the children. What courage it must have taken to visit this grieving family. I am so happy they came for at least they made the holiday seem somewhat real. Buddy came to me before the funeral and asked if Joan could be excused from coming to the funeral. She had waited nine years to finally be blessed with their first child who was due in March. I told him I didn't want her to come. She shouldn't have to see such sorrow when she should have been so happy. I absolutely did not want her to experience this sadness. I thought it was wonderful for her to come see us at Christmas. They just made everything so normal and the children were thrilled with their gifts. I am grateful to them for their support. I can't even begin to explain what life is like after the death of a child. You feel as though your life will never be the same. If it were a physical pain, it would kill you. It took a long time for me to adjust to life again but I had two children, I was pregnant and had a husband and mother who were suffering as much as I was. I wondered what I could have done in my lifetime to make God hate me so much to give me a child and then take her away. I was quite bitter.

When we took the lessons to join the Mormon Church, the missionaries told us of how some spirits are so perfect and only needed to come to earth so that they could gain a body, and didn't need to be tested. A huge burden was lifted off my shoulders as I now had a reason for her leaving us. Now in our golden years I know it will not be long before Huey and I will hold her again and she will have the parents she has waited for.

Joan and Buddy's House in Ramsey

Joan and Buddy had a lovely home in New Jersey and we took Mama there so often. It was mainly in the summer so Mama could sit outside and admire the trees, bushes and the lovely flowers. She loved being there as we were all so welcome and they treated her so tenderly.

We had many outdoor meals and delicious meals indoors in the colder weather. I remember when he made a good dinner. He loved to cook and made fabulous food. Buddy, I think, was the only one in the family who cooked exactly like Mama. I was a good cook, because Mama lived with us, but there were some things he could duplicate perfectly. He could cook everything Mama made to perfection.

He liked to cook fancy foods for us too. He made goose one Christmas and another time he made duck. He then taught me how to prepare a duck dinner and I did very well. Our family tradition is to have Prime Rib every Christmas like Mama did. After she was gone, I was a little intimidated about how long to cook the meat and would call Buddy every year for instructions. Now my children call me and also my nephew, Danny Rozak. I think it is wonderful because Mama wanted the tradition to be passed down.

Joan was so good to my mother. She did everything she could to make her feel comfortable and wanted. They took her up to Deerfield, Massachusetts to stay with them for a while. She was very thoughtful. When our son, Dan, was born she came to see him and brought along a gift for Lori. Lori was so thrilled. I learned a lesson from her. I never gave a new baby a gift without one for the other child as I realized how happy Lori was, and most children were left out when people came with baby gifts.

The day we moved into our house in Warwick, New York, she traveled an hour from Ramsey and brought us a big package of all the things you need the first day in a new house. We had all the necessities so we could eat and get the house ready without hunting through boxes.

They were happy times and I am glad I have the memories and now you will also. Buddy loved Joan and my mother with all his heart. He actually loved all of us and would have done anything to help if we needed it.

LYNCH FAMILY REUNION

In the summer of 1966, Buddy and Joan were living in Ramsey with their two children, Matthew who was five and Christina who was 1 ½ at the time. They had a nice home and a sizable lot and they decided to have a Lynch family reunion. Buddy invited his brothers Eddie and Jimmy and his four sisters, Peggy, Mary, Dena and Bootsie (Florence) and their families. Jack Purcell, Mary's husband, came and brought his mother and father. Jack Lynch, a cousin who worked for the NYPD, had to work that day and couldn't make the reunion, but his friend Deedee came and brought Jack's granddaughter Georgia. It was a beautiful summer day and Buddy and Joan provided a great feast for all of us.

Buddy bought a side of beef and decided to roast the entire piece of meat in the ground! He dug a hole deep enough and wide enough to bury a body, it must have taken him all the previous day to do this, start a big fire in the hole and then cover it with a piece of culvert pipe the night before the reunion. The next morning, the pit was uncovered and the beef was placed in the pit, which by this time was red hot. He skewered the beef with a metal pole into cavities he made the day before in the sides of the hole so the meat could be suspended over the ground and cook properly all the way around. He placed big pans under the meat to catch the drippings to make gravy. He then put the culvert pipe back over the hole and covered the whole thing with dirt and let the beef cook for about 8 hours.

We all gathered around when Buddy thought it was time to remove the beef. I remember helping with Jimmy and Eddie and Buddy to shovel off the dirt and then remove the culvert pipe, which was red hot. We looked down into the hole and the walls were all red, the heat surged out and we had to step back and wait a while before we could grab the bar and pull the meat out of the hole. Buddy had never done this before so he was very apprehensive about the meat having cooked properly. It sure smelled like it was done and when we began to carve the meat it was obvious to everyone that the meat was done just right. It was delicious!

Along with the beef, Buddy and Joan provided a huge supply of fresh corn on the cob which the children had a great time shucking. It was a great dinner and everyone had a wonderful reunion that was talked about for many years.

Our reunion was the last time all seven of us were together. We did keep in touch by phone and visiting. I feel blessed to have lived with a wonderful family and to have been brought up during these years in the Bronx. I have lost my three brothers and my sister Mary and miss them very much. I remember all the good times we had together.

Christina Lynch-Hilgenberg

Made in the USA
Lexington, KY
18 December 2015